Copyright Information:

Copyright 2018 by Mike Roberts

All rights reserved. No part of this book may be reproduced, distributed, transmitted, stored in a retrieval system or used in any form or by any means, whether electronic, mechanical or digital, except as may be expressly permitted by applicable copyright laws or as expressly allowed by the publisher or the author in writing.

Publisher Information:

Published by Smart Consumer Solutions, LLC, 601 Van Ness Ave, STE E869 San Francisco, CA 94102.

Disclaimer:

All of the information contained in this publication is true and accurate according to the best information available to me at the time of publication. Please understand, however, that laws and credit industry practices and procedures are constantly evolving; so you should independently update laws, practices and facts before you take action. I do not accept any responsibility for errors or mistakes of any kind, or for any damages or losses that might result from the use of any information provided.

Also, I am not a lender, a collection agent or a credit reporting agency. I am not an accountant or an attorney, and nothing in these materials is intended as professional advice. It is personal opinion only. I am providing it to you without any warranties or guarantees whatsoever. To obtain advice as to the tax or legal consequences of any action covered in these materials, or any action that you might consider based on these materials, you should consult an attorney, an accountant, or both. What I have tried to do here is simply offer solid, useful information that I have obtained through my own personal and business experience. Any action you choose to take based on any information that I provide, including forms and other attachments, is entirely your responsibility.

IMPORTANT: READ THIS FIRST!

Remember to access your member dashboard located here:
www.thecreditsolutionprogram.com/members/login

We also highly recommend joining our Facebook Group here:
www.facebook.com/groups/creditsolutionprogram

This group is where thousands of members help each other with insight and advice. Often you'll find others with the exact problem you've been struggling with to help you along the right path. It's also where you'll find all the latest tips and tricks that haven't made it into the latest edition of the book yet.

If you're not into Facebook, that's ok you can still join and participate in our group. You do not need to "use" Facebook, just create a new account and join the group, and then only log in when you would like to participate. If the name on your Facebook account is different than the name you used to purchase, then please send an email to **support@thecreditsolutionprogram.com** to let us know so you will still be approved.

If you have a question about your credit that is not covered in this book, the best place to ask is in our Facebook group. You will get the best answer there and you'll usually get feedback from a lot of people.

For other questions regarding billing, account access, etc. send an email to **support@thecreditsolutionprogram.com** for help.

TABLE OF CONTENTS

How to Use the Credit Solution Program.. 4
Section I: Understanding Your Credit 6
    Chapter 1: The *REAL* Cost of Bad Credit...................................... 7
        The Story of Jack and Jim... 8
        Is This the End of the Bad News? Not Quite. 14
    Chapter 2: How Does Your "Credit" Actually Work? 18
        The Players... 18
    You (the Borrower) 18
        Your Lenders (Original Creditors, or OCs) 19
        Collection Agencies (CAs).. 21
        Credit Reporting Agencies (CRAs) 23
        The Federal Government 29
        The Players' Competing Incentives.................................. 30
Section II: Credit Reports & Credit Scores.. 32
    Chapter 3: How to Get Your Credit Records 33
    Chapter 4: Exactly What's In Your Credit Report? 34
        Your Identity, or Personal Information............................. 35
        Your Credit Accounts.. 35
        Your Public Information 37
        Consumer Statement (Personal Statement) 38
        The Summary 38
        Inquiries... 39
    Chapter 5: Understanding Your Credit Score.............................. 47
        Some Questions and Answers 47
        The Five "Credit Factors".. 53
Section III: What You Can Do to Improve Your Credit............................ 59
    Chapter 6: Steps to Raise Your Score 60
        Step 1—Manage Your Payment History.......................... 60
        Step 2—Control Your Use of Available Credit................. 62
        Step 3—Age Your Accounts... 64
        Step 4—Mix Your Credit Types.. 65
        Step 5—Minimize New Credit.. 67
    Chapter 7: How to Remove Negative Items from Your Report... 69
        Identifying Your Negative Items 71
        Removing Items Marked 30-60 Days Late 72
        Removing Items Marked 90-150 Days Late 75
        Removing "Collections" Items That Remain Unpaid........ 79
            A CA Reported the Collections Item. 81
            The OC Reported the Collections Item. 86
        Removing "Collections" Items That Are Paid 86

  Removing Errors from Your Report 87
  Keeping Negative Items Off Your Report 92
  Final Thoughts 93
Appendix: Forms and Samples... 95
 Sample Goodwill Letter 1... 96
 Sample Goodwill Letter 2... 98
 Sample Goodwill Letter 3... 100
 Sample FCBA Evidence Request 101
 Sample Validation Request 1 103
 Wollman FTC Opinion Letter.. 105
 Cass FTC Opinion Letter.. 107
 Sample Investigation Request...................................... 109
 Sample Validation Request 2 111

How to Use the Credit Solution Program...

Congratulations on starting down the road to improving your personal credit. As you probably know, I hear from thousands of people with poor credit on a very regular basis, and I interact with them through emails, chats and comment forums. If there's one thing I've learned for sure, it's that most people with credit trouble know very well that their lives would be happier if somehow they could make their credit better. Still, many don't take action. They see the problem, but they don't try to solve it.

You're different. Not only do you know it's important for you to get your credit into better shape; but you're doing something about it—right now. You've taken the initiative to buy this book, and now you're about to start down the path to a better financial future. You've already set yourself apart, and if you follow the steps that I outline for you, you're going to succeed in improving your credit. The keys to your success (the tools you need) are right here in this book.

It's divided into three parts:

1. **Part I – Understanding Your Credit.** This is a detailed review of the reasons why good credit is important to you. It also covers the companies, institutions and players in the financial credit industry and how the things they do, or don't do, affect your credit standing.

2. **Part II – Credit Reports & Credit Scores—the Two Parts of the Puzzle.** This is where I teach you how to understand your credit reports and your credit scores. I take you through all the components of both reports and scores, and show you in detail how they relate to each other. I introduce you to the laws that are on your side, take you through certain steps designed to improve you credit, and show you the behaviors you have to avoid if you want to keep it healthy.

3. **Part III – What You Can Do to Improve Your Credit, Starting Now.** Here I show you the mechanics of mending your credit— how to use the weapons that the law makes available to you. I show you changes you can make in your personal financial life that will help your credit going forward. Finally, your credit record almost certainly contains negative items that are causing you

serious financial harm. There are ways to get them removed, and this is where I show you how to do it.

I strongly recommend that you read the book all the way through once and that you then go back and make sure you understand Sections I and II before you start using the tools and taking the action steps described in Section III. Here's why: It's vitally important that you UNDERSTAND all the ways that poor credit can cheat you out of a happy, fulfilling life (this will keep you motivated and inspired); and it's absolutely crucial that you find out

- Who you're dealing with out there in the credit world (the various lenders, the collection agencies, and the credit reporting agencies), and

- What motivates them to do the things they do.

Once you know who the important players are, and how they relate to one another in the complex financial credit system they've created, you'll dramatically increase your chances for success.

Also, remember that a better life is waiting for you at the other end of this program. Once you improve your personal credit, you'll probably be applying for loans, using credit cards, and generally dealing with lenders for a long time to come. It only makes sense to take advantage of this opportunity to gain an understanding of how the consumer credit system works.

Finally, as you read and work your way through this program, please remember that I created it for you, and I want it to be as accurate and helpful as possible. So . . . if you have any corrections, changes, or suggestions, I really would like to hear from you!

PS. Just one more thing before we get into the material: You wouldn't believe how many hundreds of hours it takes to write, edit, and publish material like this...and so, as a favor to me, I am going to ask that you NOT copy these files or documents for others. If you know someone who would benefit from this book and its supplementary materials, just give them my email or website address and I'll be happy to take their order. Thanks!

Section I:
UNDERSTANDING YOUR CREDIT

Chapter 1:
THE _REAL_ COST OF BAD CREDIT

Before we get into the details of exactly what "credit" is, and how you can improve yours, I want to cover the reasons why having "good credit" is so vitally important. To some extent this is going to involve talking about some pretty scary stuff, and at first it might sound like I'm inventing things just to motivate you. I promise you that the truth is terrifying enough; there's no need to make up anything.

The fact is that "bad credit" can creep into your life and cause you all kinds of harm, sometimes in ways that you would never suspect. It can damage aspects of your life that most people would never imagine.

So what is "bad credit" exactly? Well, as you probably know, each of us has something called a "credit score." If it's high enough (say, above 720), then we have "good credit"; and if it's low enough (below 620), our credit is bad.

> For the moment, I'm not going to get into all the details of exactly what a credit score is, what it's based on, how it is calculated, who calculates it, and so on.
>
> These things are all important, and we'll cover all of them later, chapter and verse, I promise.
>
> For now, let's just accept the idea that it's good to have a score of 720 or better, and it's not good at all to have one below 620.

At this early stage, I want to focus on just one thing: All the ways that bad credit can cause terrible harm to good people.

The Story of Jack and Jim

Two Friends on Parallel Tracks:

Let me introduce you to Jack and Jim. Now Jack and Jim aren't real people, but their experiences are very real, maybe very familiar. If you bought this book, you're probably not Jack (you'll see why in a moment); but you might very well be Jim, or you might know someone just like him.

Jack is 23 years old, a college graduate, and a promising young engineer. He has a great job with a good company and his future is bright. His buddy Jim is also 23. He graduated from the same college as Jack, and he works with Jack at the same company for the same pay. His future is also bright.

All in all, Jack and Jim are almost identical... almost! Unfortunately for Jim, their pasts are very different in one crucial detail.

- **What Jack's Dad Taught Him:** When Jack was 16, he and his dad had a long talk about the birds and the bees; and Jack's dad added something to the conversation that most dads don't cover. He figured since he had Jack's attention anyway, he would use it to talk to Jack about how credit works. He listened carefully to the discussion about credit. He listened, learned, and he didn't forget.

- **What Jim's Dad Didn't Teach Him:** Jim's dad, on the other hand, just gave Jim a book on the facts of life and asked Jim to let him know if he had any questions. The book didn't cover credit, and Jim's dad never mentioned it. Now this doesn't mean that Jim's dad isn't a good guy. He's a good person and a good father; but like many of us, he just didn't understand the importance of teaching his son about credit. Jim and his dad always had a great relationship, and they often went hunting and fishing together; but to this day, Jim is clueless about how credit works and why good credit is important.

Their First New Cars:

Fast forward to the present day. Both Jack and Jim have started to enjoy their well-earned success. They've decided that the time has come for each to buy his first new car. Because they both come from the same town, went to the same schools, and work at similar jobs at the same company, they have similar tastes in cars. They've both picked out the same model. It's going for $22,750, everything included, and they both have $2,750 for a down payment. Unfortunately, their parallel tracks end right here. They are NOT going to have the same buying experience.

Jack is going to enjoy buying his first new car; Jim isn't.

- Jack has carefully managed his credit, just as his father advised. As a result, the sales manager at the dealership has just told Jack that his "credit score" is an enviable 750.

- Jim, on the other hand, has not found his father's lessons about hunting and fishing useful in matters of finance, and he has done nothing to maintain his credit score over his early adult life. Even so, he has tried to pay his bills on time and as a result his personal credit score comes in at 650, only 100 points lower than Jack's. Not awful; but not good either. Here's the difference this 100 points is going to make.

Both Jack and Jim are going to be financing $20,000 of the purchase price over a period of five years, and this is where the rubber meets the road (pun intended). Jack's 750 credit score qualifies him for a nice low interest rate of 5% and a monthly payment of $377. Jim's not-so-good score of 650, however, forces him into an interest rate of 8% and a monthly payment of $406.

> OUCH! Assuming they both make payments on time and pay off their cars in five years, Jim will end up paying $384 more for his car in the first year than Jack pays for his, and $1,740 more over five years.
>
> If nothing changes (that is if interest rates stay the same, if there is no inflation, and if Jack doesn't sit Jim down and teach him something about how personal credit really works), then the two buddies will probably repeat this performance ten times over the rest of their driving lives. If they do, the numbers become even more unpleasant (from Jim's point of view, of course).

Here's a grid that illustrates Jim's financial pain:

Loan Details	Jack	Jim
Credit Score	750	650
Interest Rate	5.0%	8.0%
Loan Amount	$20,000	$20,000
Monthly Payment (based on 5-yr loan)	$377	$406
5 Years of Payments	$22,620	$24,360
Lifetime of Payments on 10 Car Loans	$226,200	$243,600
Cost of Bad Credit	--	**$17,400**

The story of Jack and Jim doesn't end here. There's a lot more financial hardship in store for Jim.

Their Credit Cards

Jack and Jim are both smart and hardworking, and they're going to succeed at work. As their incomes increase, each will decide that he could benefit from the convenience of a credit card. The credit card companies are always trolling for new customers, and it won't take them long to find out about these two up-and-coming lads. Jack and Jim will be deluged with credit card offers, and they'll do what most people do (according to national averages)—they'll each start carrying at least three cards. If one is good, three should be great, right? Well, maybe; it depends on whether you're Jack or Jim.

In Jack's case, his 750 credit score will get him an interest rate of "only" 9.5% for each of his cards. That's pretty good as credit card interest goes. Jim won't qualify for a rate anywhere close to that. Here's where Jim's 100 point deficit will make a huge difference. He'll have to make do with an interest rate of 19.5%. Jack won't be worried, because he'll tell himself what we all tell ourselves in this situation—"The rate won't matter because I won't keep much of a balance on the card."

> Unfortunately for Jack, what he tells himself probably won't turn out to be true. In fact, throughout their lives both Jack and Jim likely will carry average balances of $3,000 for each card, and this is about on par with an average total balance per person for the US population that carries credit card debt.

Let's see how those balances and interest rates are going to work out over the long term...

Loan Details	Jack	Jim
Credit Score	750	650
Interest Rate	9.5%	19.5%
Balance Amount per card	$3,000	$3,000
Annual Interest per card	$285	$585
Annual Interest - 3 cards	$855	$1,755
Lifetime Interest on 3 cards (50 yrs)	$42,750	$87,750
Cost of Bad Credit	--	**$45,000**

Yes, I know; this is really bad news for Jim. But there's worse yet waiting for him.

Their Houses:

Jack and Jim are intent on living the American dream, and as we all know, that involves owning a home. If they follow the average path, they'll both buy relatively small houses to start out, and live in them for about ten years. Then they'll trade up to bigger, more elaborate places with more amenities. They'll stay in these upper scale homes, pay them off, and live in them for the rest of their lives.

Let's assume some average home price numbers (homes might be going for more or less where you live), and some historically average interest rates, and take a look at the long-term consequences of Jim's credit score.

First House	Jack	Jim
Credit Score	750	650
Mortgage Rate	5.0%	8.0%
Mortgage Amount	$250,000	$250,000
Monthly Payment (based on 30-yr mtg)	$1,342	$1,834
10 Years of Payments	$161,040	$220,080
Cost of Bad Credit	--	**$59,040**

Second House	Jack	Jim
Credit Score	750	650
Mortgage Rate	5.0%	8.0%
Mortgage Amount	$450,000	$450,000
Monthly Payment (based on 30-yr mtg)	$2,416	$3,302
10 Years of Payments	$869,760	$1,188,720
Cost of Bad Credit	--	**$318,960**

These are absolutely killer numbers. Over 40 years of home ownership, Jim will pay out a breathtaking $378,000 more than Jack to live in exactly the same two homes. In most places, that's enough money to buy a really nice home for cash, and never send a single payment to a mortgage bank.

OK... At this point we're almost ready to let Jack and Jim get on with their lives, but first let's review the total cost to Jim.

Itemized Costs	Jim's Cost of Bad Credit
Auto Loans	$17,400
Credit Cards	$45,000
Mortgage - First House	$55,040
Mortgage - Second House	$318,960
Total Cost of Bad Credit	**$436,400**

Look... $436,400 is a pretty high cost to pay for poor credit, especially when you consider that Jim's credit isn't awful—it's just not as good as Jack's. But the reality of Jim's situation is actually even worse.

Consider this: The $436,400 Jim is going to need to pay all this extra interest isn't going to fall out of the sky. No one is going to give it to him. Jim is going to have to work hard at his company and actually _earn_ all the money he'll be paying out in extra interest over his lifetime. If he had credit as good as Jack's, he could invest that money as he earned it instead of paying it through the nose to his creditors.

> He probably wouldn't do that with all of it (he'd probably spend some of it on vacations, hobbies, school tuition for the kids, a faster car, a bigger TV—you know, ratchet up the lifestyle a little); but let's assume for the moment that he would invest all the extra interest in a retirement savings account of some kind.

If Jim invested all the money he's going to spend on extra interest, here's what he would have down the road, assuming very conservative investment rates:

Jim's Lost Investment Value	Totals
Value of Extra Car Loan Interest Invested at 2.75% Over 50 Years	$38,829
Value of Extra Credit Card Interest Invested at 2.75% Over 50 Years	$100,419
Value of Extra Mortgage Interest on First House Invested at 2.75% over 50 Years	$226,408
Value of Extra Mortgage Interest on Second House Invested at 2.75% over 40 Years	$686,226
Total Value of Lost Investments	**$1,051,882**

$1,051,882? Yes, that's the number, and it is a very great deal of money. Now granted, Jim would have to be a real saint to religiously invest every single dollar of the cost of his 650 score over his projected life, but this grid should give you an idea of just how much self-inflicted pain poor credit can cause.

Even if Jim invested only half of the money, he would have enough to live a very different lifestyle from the one that's in store for him, and he would have something left over to retire at a reasonable age in the bargain. In fact, that's exactly what Jack will do; and because they're close friends, Jim will have to watch Jack do it.

In the years to come, Jim and Jack will continue working at the same company at similar jobs, and they will make the same money; but their lives will be very different. As time goes by, Jim will be left to ponder a couple of lingering questions:

1. "Why is Jack's lifestyle so much better than mine? Where does Jack get all this extra money? Did someone die and leave it to him? Is he stealing it?"

2. "Why is Jack able to retire early and keep living the high life while I have to keep slaving away with no prospect of retirement in sight?"

This is going to be tough for Jim to take (it would be for anybody). As their financial paths take the two friends farther and farther apart, Jim might not handle it well. This is the kind of thing that can lead a person to develop an ulcer from stress. Maybe their friendship will survive it, and maybe it won't. We'll leave them here and wish them the best of luck. Jim is going to need it.

Is This the End of the Bad News? Not Quite.

Let's review where we are with all the ways bad credit can harm good, well-meaning people. We've learned quite a bit from the struggles of Jim.

Borrowing: If your credit isn't up to par,

1. You'll pay more for car loans,

2. You'll pay a great deal more for your credit cards, and

3. You'll pay a frightening additional amount in mortgage interest—literally, a fortune.

In fact, borrowing of every conceivable kind will cost you more—a lot more.

Lifestyle: The cost of poor credit isn't just in the additional money you have to spend to get by—it's also in the THINGS YOU DON'T GET TO DO.

1. If you don't qualify for the best rates on loans and credit cards, you don't get to invest the extra money spent.

2. If you don't qualify for the best rates on loans and credit cards, you don't get to buy nice things with that money—things you'd like to have for yourself and your family.

Lost Opportunities: If you have poor credit, then many good opportunities almost certainly will pass you by—usually very quietly and without any explanation.

1. Bad credit can cost you the chance to rent in a nice neighborhood or in an apartment complex that's safe for you and your kids.

2. Bad credit can cost you the job you've been looking for—maybe the breakout job that you desperately need to get your life on track.

3. Bad credit can cost you a favorable rate on any kind of insurance, including car insurance.

Health and Happiness: There's one more, very important aspect to all this that we haven't yet discussed, and that's this—poor credit is sneaky. Its effects creep in slowly over time. The bad things happen little by little, and as the money dribbles away, you tend not to focus on it. That's because it doesn't call attention to itself. It's quiet.

> It's as if your bank account is a bucket with a hole in the bottom. You're trying to fill it from the top, and all the while money is draining out through the hole that you don't see.
>
> It's very hard to fill that bucket when you're constantly fighting against the drain of a bad credit score.

Don't forget that you have a right to the "Pursuit of Happiness." (It's in The Declaration of Independence, after all.) You don't have a right to BE happy; but you certainly do have a right always to be working on it. Believe me, it's almost impossible to work on being happy if you have poor credit.

Even if somehow you're able to remain focused and you devote all your energy to leading a happy, satisfying life, your chances for success are much lower with poor credit. That's because everything becomes harder than it has to be. Poor credit creates a dark cloud that can simply hang over your life and follow you around. It's an anvil around your neck, a weight that just drags you down. Many experts believe that stress from financial pressure is one of the most important causes of:

- Divorce (it's hard not to fight about money when it is really scarce),

- Addictive behavior (as in, drowning your sorrows),

- Aggressive behavior (some people can't help taking their problems out on others),

- Depression (the pressure can build up inside and color how you feel about everything), and

- Certain serious physical illnesses (the stress can literally eat away at you and cause physical harm).

I think those folks are right who point to financial stress as a leading cause of these serious social problems.

You're about to start down a road that is going to require some effort on your part. You're going to need some diligence, some energy, and some tenacity. I hope you'll keep in mind the struggles of the fictitious characters we've covered, and I hope their stories will inspire you, help you stay focused, and allow you to avoid the consequences of failure.

I want you to improve your personal credit standing for all the reasons I've covered in this first chapter. I can't promise you that good credit will bring you happiness and success, but I absolutely can promise you that it will dramatically increase the chances that you'll achieve both.

Chapter 2:
HOW DOES YOUR "CREDIT" ACTUALLY WORK?

Your personal credit picture is part of a huge, complex financial system. In this chapter, I'm going to introduce you to this system, simplify it for you, and let you in on how the component parts work.

The Players

The system is made up of the following players:

1. You (the borrower),

2. Your lenders (aka, your creditors—the people you borrow from),

3. The Collection Agencies (the people who chase you when you don't pay),

4. The Credit Reporting Agencies (the people who maintain your credit records), and

5. The Federal Government (the folks who pass federal laws that regulate the personal financial services industry).

These five parties, working together (though NOT with the same goals or motivations), create your personal credit standing. Here's how it works.

You (the Borrower)

Let's start with the person you know best—you. If you're like 99% of the population, you've borrowed money in the past and you'll borrow again sometime soon. Most of us, in fact, borrow money early and often, and we do it dozens of times throughout our adult lives.

You borrow every time you sign up for a credit card, take out a student loan, buy a car on credit, take out a mortgage to purchase a home, or just agree to take advantage of the "No Payments 'til Spring" offer at your local furniture store.

- You can borrow from a bank, a credit union, a finance company, a credit card company, or a retail outlet, and the list doesn't end there.

- You can borrow and put up security (like when you promise to let the finance company repossess your car if you don't pay the loan), or you can simply borrow on your signature (like when you sign up for a credit card).

For most of us, borrowing is pretty much a fact of modern life. It's inevitable.

Now whenever you borrow, you sign an agreement in which you promise to repay. Sometimes this agreement is formal and detailed (like a credit card agreement or a mortgage loan contract), and sometimes it isn't; but it's always there. There's always a contract between you and the company or institution that is providing the money. In this book we're going to call these companies "original creditors" or "OCs" for short.

Regardless of whether the contract is simple or complicated, it always boils down to these basic elements:

1. Your written promise to repay the money under certain terms and conditions,

2. The lender's right to sue you in court if you don't repay the money as promised, and

3. If the loan is secured, the lender's right to repossess whatever it is that you bought with the money—your car, your house, your boat, whatever.

Once you enter into a borrowing agreement with a lender, you either make all the payments on time, in the amounts that the contract calls for, or you don't. As time goes on, you build up a personal credit history that the system uses to determine your credit standing—to determine whether you have "good credit" or "bad credit."

Your Lenders (Original Creditors, or OCs)

Now, as you make payments to your lenders, your lenders keep track of how you're doing. In fact, they pay a lot of attention to how you're doing, and they keep a record of it. This isn't shocking. They want their money, and they want it on time. They're in the business of loaning money at interest, and when you don't pay, or when you pay late, it cuts into their profits. They hate that.

So, if you get behind in your payments, you can count on hearing from your lender. At first, the reminder might be gentle.

> As in,
>
> "Hey _____, Did you forget about us this month? If you've already sent your payment, please disregard this friendly reminder."

If you pay right away, they'll leave you alone; if you don't, the notices quickly become much more urgent in tone. If you get too far behind, you'll get a notice that runs along these lines:

> "You are now _____ months past due on your account. If the amount due, $_____, is not paid in full within 10 days of the date of this notice, the account will be turned over to collections."

These notices might come from your lender directly (say your bank or your finance company) or they might come from what is called a "loan servicer."

A loan servicer is simply an independent company that sells administrative resources to lenders. Lenders hire these companies to keep track of payments, send out notices, and generally handle the day-to-day business of dealing with borrowers. Either the lender or its loan servicer normally will make the initial attempts to persuade you to pay if you get behind. The notices you see in the boxes above both came from either the lender or the loan servicer.

But if you don't pay after a certain number of notices, the lender will move things to a whole new level—it will turn your account over to a collection agency. This is never a good thing from the borrower's point of view.

Collection Agencies (CAs)

Think of a collection agency as a hired gun. It isn't a lender or a loan servicer. It's an independent company that exists to do only one thing—to collect money from people who are seriously delinquent on their payments. If a lender (or its servicer) finds that it isn't able to get a delinquent account back on track through its own efforts, it doesn't just forget about the debt. Instead, it turns to a specialist—the collection agency, or "CA."

A lender will get a collection agency involved in a delinquent account in one of two ways:

1. It will simply hire the CA to collect the account and pay the CA for its services.

    a. Often the CA's compensation has two parts: The first is a flat fee, paid up front; the second is a percentage of any amounts that might later be collected. This way, the CA gets paid something for its efforts whether it is successful in collecting or not.

    b. Sometimes the lender just pays the CA a straight commission, and with this arrangement, the CA doesn't get paid unless if collects something.

With either arrangement, the lender continues to be the owner of the contract, and the CA is said to be a "third party agency." If you're the borrower, you still owe the money to the lender, not the CA, even though it's the CA that is contacting you about the delinquent payments.

2. Or the lender might simply sell the original contract to the CA.

    a. This is more likely to be the case if the account is many months, maybe even years past due. In such situations, the CA buys all of the lender's rights in the contract for pennies on the dollar. When this happens, the CA is said to be a "first party agency." Later, you'll see why it can be important for you to know if you're dealing with a "third party" or "first party" CA.

    b. It isn't uncommon for the sale of a loan contract to happen more than once. Sometimes a delinquent account will be sold from CA to CA two or three times (with each successive CA paying substantially less for the contract). Once your original lender sells your contract to a CA, you owe the money to the CA that currently owns that contract, not to the original lender.

> "Wait a minute," you might be thinking, "can an OC just sell my contract to a collection agent without my permission?"
>
> The answer is almost always yes. Most loan contracts have a clause in the fine print that allows the original creditor to assign (sell) the contract to a third party. Basically, you agree to this in advance.

Collecting money from people who don't have it, or don't want to pay, is a tough business, and collection agencies behave accordingly. They are often successful in collecting money that banks can't collect because they are willing to use tactics and practices that lenders (OCs) normally don't employ. In fact, some of these companies have a long history of abusive conduct. In years past, it wasn't uncommon for them to

- Call borrowers (debtors) repeatedly, at all hours of the day or night,

- Use abusive and harassing language in speaking with debtors,

- Call the borrower's employer about the debt, or threaten to call the employer,

- Call the borrower's friends or family about the debt, or threaten to call them,

- Threaten the debtor with a lawsuit when they had no intention of filing one, or

- Threaten the debtor with criminal prosecution, arrest or jail (there isn't now, and there has never been, any legal basis for criminal action or arrest based on a debt).

Much of this nonsense is in the past. Because of reforms imposed by federal laws (which we'll be covering in detail later), these practices now are illegal; and CAs can incur substantial fines if they lapse into some of their former habits. Even so, it's important to remember their history, and to keep in mind that not all CAs are as conscientious as they should be about following the law.

Even though CAs behave better these days than they used to, it's safe to say that they typically take a much more aggressive attitude toward borrowers than do lenders (OCs).

Credit Reporting Agencies (CRAs)

OK. Now it's time to talk about the very important guys in the back room (figuratively speaking, of course). These are the people nobody ever sees--the number crunchers, the bean counters, the folks wearing the green eyeshades. In reality, the "green eyeshade" image couldn't be further from the truth. What we're talking about here are three huge, very sophisticated, billion-dollar corporations, and they are the keepers of your credit files. They maintain, and continually update, your credit records, my credit records, and the credit records of just about every person in the western world over the age of 18.

Where did these companies come from? Well, they arose to fill a need in the marketplace. In a real sense, they exist today because lenders everywhere want them to exist.

Lenders have always been interested in finding out as much as possible about borrowers in order to predict the likelihood of repayment. From the beginning, they have operated on a single principle—past behavior is the best indicator of future behavior. Put another way, they believe that if you have paid your debts promptly in the past, you probably will do so in the future; and if you haven't, you probably won't start now.

> This attitude among lenders isn't going to change any time soon. It's just human nature. If your friend Charlie asks you to spot him $50 until payday, you'll probably do it if he has repaid you in the past. If he stiffed you last time, or didn't pay on time, you'll hold on to your $50.

Early in the days of consumer credit, each lender would do its best to research the payment histories of loan applicants, but they didn't have a good system. The process was haphazard, expensive, and unreliable. The reality in those days was that if you defaulted on a loan in Virginia, for example, you could move to Maine and borrow more money. The bank in Maine might not know that you recently failed to make your payments in Virginia.

> It wasn't that they didn't want to know, of course; they desperately wanted to know. It's just that they had no quick, inexpensive way to find out.
>
> There was no place they could go to get solid information about your repayment habits for all your old, out-of-state loans.

You see where this is going, right? This isn't the kind of problem that remains unsolved indefinitely—especially when the people with the problem are big banks, finance companies, and other institutions with boatloads of money. Before too long the old, weak system gave way to one in which all lenders everywhere started "reporting" all payment activity on all their loans to a central place (actually three central places—information clearing houses, if you will).

These clearing houses (these days we call them Credit Reporting Agencies, or CRAs) saw a chance to build enormous, extremely profitable businesses. They each hired thousands of staff, built huge bureaucracies, and installed technology that enables them to amass and keep track of an unbelievable amount of detailed information on millions of consumers and their loans.

When the dust settled, there were (and there still are) three major companies that now are the custodians of consumer credit information both nationally and worldwide. How does this system work? Let's look in on a fictitious borrower to find out:

Sharon's Loan

Sharon is an enterprising high school grad who has just turned 18. Until now, she has never borrowed a dime, but now she's out of high school and soon she'll be off to a nearby community college. She's going to live at home and commute, because she can't afford to live on campus, but she needs a car. She finds a pretty sharp, light blue, six-year-old Corolla for $6,000 and she finances $5,000. She's psyched (her first car—awesome), but she might not be so excited if she knew what she has set in motion behind the scenes. A series of events now unfolds involving her lender and the CRAs.

- Her lender notifies all three CRAs about her loan and provides a lot of very detailed information about her and the transaction (her name, her address, her social security number, the opening balance on the loan, the date of the loan, the nature of the loan, etc.). Each CRA opens a credit file with Sharon's name on it.

- From time to time, as Sharon makes timely payments, her lender reports the excellent status of the loan to the CRAs. They put the information into Sharon's file as it comes in.

- As Sharon falls behind for a couple of payments (she has a long bout with the flu and can't work very many hours at her part time job), her lender reports to all three CRAs that the account is 60 days past due. They all put this information in Sharon's file as well. Sharon starts feeling better and gets back on track with her payments.

   Before long, Sharon sees that she isn't going to be able to make ends meet without a student loan. She applies for one for $6,000 with a different lender, and she gets it. This new lender does exactly what the car loan lender did. It reports this new loan to all the CRAs, and just like the other lender, provides all kinds of detailed information about Sharon and the loan. The CRAs put all this new data in Sharon's file.

- Until Sharon graduates, she won't have to start repaying this student loan, but the fact that it exists as a future obligation for Sharon goes to the CRAs on day one and becomes part of her file. Once she starts making payments, the lender will make periodic reports to the CRAs on how she is doing, and these reports, like all the others, will go into her file.

And so it will go with Sharon. As she moves along with her life, her lenders will continue to send updates to the CRAs about her loans. If she does a great job of paying everything on time, her records should reflect that; if she doesn't, her records should show that too.

> I say "should" because, as we've already noted with our friend Bob, it is very common for these CRA files to contain errors. Some of these errors can have disastrous consequences (for the consumer, of course, not for the CRA).

The point of this process is obvious. As we've already discussed, Sharon probably will borrow several times in the years to come. Every time she applies for credit, her new lender will simply contact the CRAs and ask, "What have you got on Sharon?" The lender will pay an "inquiry fee" to the CRA—that's how they make their money—and in return the CRAs will grab the information they have on file for Sharon and supply it to the lender.

> The information that the CRAs supply to Sharon's lenders will take two forms:
>
> 1. A detailed credit report that lists all of her loans and describes her payment history on each one, and
>
> 2. A "credit score," which is a three-digit number that is calculated based on the information in the credit report.

Depending on how good a job Sharon does in repaying her various loans on time, the information that the CRAs report back on Sharon (her credit report and her credit score) will show that

1. Her credit is good (she has an unblemished report and a high score), in which case the lender will be happy to loan Sharon more money;

2. Her credit isn't great, but it's not awful (she has a report with some negative marks, and a mediocre score), in which case the lender will make the loan but will insist on terms that are much less favorable than she might like; or

3. Her credit is bad (her report is messy and she has a low score), in which case the lender probably won't make the loan at all.

So, in the immortal words of Butch Cassidy, "Who are those guys?" Who are these mega-companies who now keep tabs on all of us? Who are these people who for a fee hand out information to lenders that can have such enormous consequences for all of us?

The answer: They are Equifax, Experian and TransUnion (for some reason, they all have weird names).

Equifax: Founded in 1899 in Atlanta as the Retail Credit Corporation, Experian is the oldest major consumer credit company in the world. Historically, it has gathered, managed, and sold credit information to anyone with money. In fact, its corporate practices are often cited as a major factor in the passage of the federal "Fair Credit Reporting Act" in 1970. This law regulates the collection, distribution, and use of consumer credit information and is considered the foundation of financial consumer protection in the U.S.

Experian: Experian was founded in 1980 and is headquartered in Dublin, Ireland. Originally named "CCN Systems", the company has grown by acquiring local and regional credit organizations. The acquisition of "TRW Information Services" provided much of its current credit reporting structure.

TransUnion: TransUnion was founded in 1968 in Chicago. The company grew rapidly by acquiring city-based credit agencies. Today it is the third largest credit firm internationally and has offices worldwide.

All three of these companies are private, FOR PROFIT businesses. They operate for the purpose of making money, period. Depending on whom you ask, you might be told that these CRAs were created by Congress, that they are federal agencies, or that they are required by law to compile credit records and make them available to lenders.

> None of that is true. Congress did not create the CRAs, they are not federal agencies, and they are not part of any government. There is no legal requirement that they keep information about you.
>
> In fact, the only laws in effect that relate to these CRAs are the laws Congress passed to protect consumers from their abusive practices.

The business model of the credit bureaus is really kind of strange when you think about it. Lenders voluntarily supply the credit bureaus with information about consumers – late payments, etc. Then they later pay the CRAs to get this same information back in the form of reports.

Why does it work this way? For two very good business reasons:

1. Lenders use the CRAs as leverage to get you to pay on time. They are willing to give information to the bureaus because they know that the threat of a bad credit rating makes it more likely that you will pay them back as agreed. It's essentially a legal form of blackmail.

2. The CRAs provide a very useful service to the lenders in collecting, synthesizing, and quickly making available all this detailed information upon request. The lenders would much rather have the CRAs do all this bureaucratic work and just pay for the information when they need it.

It's important to understand that the credit bureaus don't work together. They aren't partnered in any way--in fact, they are competitors. Each tries to convince lenders to report to them and to purchase their data on consumers. Most lenders have a favorite one or two, and most of the big lenders use all three.

That's enough about the CRAs for the time being. We'll have a lot more to say about them, and their operations, in later chapters. Now we're going to move along to the fifth, and final player—the US Government.

The Federal Government

I'm listing the United States Federal Government as a player here not because it takes a day-to-day, active role in determining your credit standing (it doesn't), but because the United States Congress has passed some extremely important laws that directly influence how the other players (the lenders, the CAs and the CRAs) behave.

> In fact, these laws provide you, the borrower, with powerful weapons that you can use to protect yourself from abuse from the OCs, the CAs and the CRAs).
>
> Much of the remainder of this book will involve showing you exactly how to use these weapons.

There are three of these laws. They are all federal laws (not state) so they apply everywhere in the US. All of them are on the books for your benefit.

The Fair Credit Billing Act (FCBA):

This law is aimed at the lenders (OCs). It is part of a larger federal law (the Truth in Lending Act), and its purpose is to make sure that lenders bill their customers fairly, accurately and completely. It spells out certain consumer rights, including the right to dispute bills, and I'll show you how to use these rights to your advantage later in this program.

The Fair Debt Collection Practices Act (FDCPA):

This law regulates the collection agencies (CAs). It dictates exactly what debt collectors can and can't do, and it prohibits many of the abuses that used to be common before this law came into effect. Because of this law, CAs are now held to certain behavioral standards, and if they don't meet those standards, they are subject to fines and penalties.

Later I'm going to show you how to use this law against the CAs with a powerful tactic called Debt Validation, which involves your right to request certain specific information from the CA regarding an alleged debt.

The Fair Credit Reporting Act (FCRA):

This law zeros in on the credit reporting agencies (CRAs). It tells them what they can and can't do, and it ensures that consumers can get access to their credit reports and scores. It regulates who is allowed to acquire a consumer's report and for what reasons, and it places limits on how long information can remain on a credit report.

Finally, it recognizes that a consumer might want to dispute the information contained in his report (yes, that sounds like something we might want to do), and it prescribes exactly what a CRA must do when it receives notice that a report is being disputed. Again, I'll soon show you exactly how to use this last part to your advantage.

The Players' Competing Incentives

Let's review what we've covered so far. There are five players in the consumer credit game—you, your lenders, collection agencies, credit reporting agencies, and the government. Your goals and motives are very different from those of the other players.

You: You are probably going to borrow money in your lifetime. Your goal is to be able to borrow money when you need it.

> Your incentive is always to make sure, if you can, that your credit report casts you in the best possible light, and that your credit score is as high as possible. That way, you'll always be able to borrow on the best possible terms, and at the lowest rates.

Your Lenders: Your lenders (the OCs) are going to want to loan you money if they think you'll repay it. They are in the business of lending money, collecting interest, and making a profit. As long as they think you're going to pay the money back, they want to loan it to you at the highest interest rate possible.

> The lenders' business model is pretty simple--The higher the interest rate on any given loan, the more money they make. They can get away with charging you a higher rate when your credit report has problems and your score is lower. Therefore, their incentive is to do what they can to keep your credit rating down.

The Collection Agencies: These folks hire out to the OCs to collect on loan accounts that are in trouble. Their only concern is to bring in money. That's it. They have a history of abusive practices, and their incentive is to do whatever they can (usually within the law, but sometimes in violation of the law) to collect money for themselves or their clients—the OCs.

The Credit Reporting Agencies: Like the CAs, these CRAs work for the lenders (the OCs). They accumulate information from lenders, compile it, and sell it back to the lenders. Again, this is a pretty simple business model. Their main concern is to keep their lender clients happy.

The three CRAs all compete with each other. Their incentive is to compile negative information on consumers, and to report lower credit scores, because they know that if the information they report is negative, their client lenders make more money. They look at it this way: The more unfavorable the data they report to a lender, the more likely that lender will continue to report to them and to pay them for future "inquiries."

The US Government: Without the government, the deck is pretty much stacked against you. You're just one person. You're up against powerful banks, finance companies, credit card companies, collection agencies, and huge, billion-dollar credit reporting bureaucracies. You want your credit score to be high; your opposition wants it to be lower. They're rich and powerful and you're not. At first glance, this doesn't look like a fair fight.

Fortunately, Congress has passed some federal laws that put some powerful weapons in your hands—tools which, if used correctly, can level the playing field. In the remainder of this book, I'm going to show you exactly how to use these weapons, improve your credit standing, and make a better life for yourself.

Section II:
CREDIT REPORTS & CREDIT SCORES - THE TWO PARTS TO THE PUZZLE

Chapter 3:
HOW TO GET YOUR CREDIT RECORDS

Now that you know all the good reasons why you need to improve your credit, an d now that you know who (and what) you're up against, it's time to get copies of your records. These records consist of

1. Your Credit Report, and

2. Your Credit Score.

Each of the CRAs (Equifax, Experian and TransUnion) publishes its own version of your credit report, and each one makes its own calculation of your credit score. You need **ALL THREE** reports, and **ALL THREE** scores.

> "Why all three?" You are probably asking. "Aren't they all the same?"
>
> They're not necessarily the same. Lenders are not required to report to all three CRAs, and some just report to one or two. As a result, your three reports might be different in certain important details, and this means that your scores might be different too. This is very common.

There are several ways that you can obtain this information. It offers an opportunity to get all three of your credit reports and all three of your scores on a free trial basis (it's not the only service with this offer; it's just the one I like). Just follow these steps:

1. Go to the website: http://www.tcsp.link/CR

2. Follow the instructions on the page to obtain a current copy of your credit report and score.

Chapter 4:
EXACTLY WHAT'S IN YOUR CREDIT REPORT?

Learning how to read your credit report (and understand what's in it) will be absolutely essential to using the weapons we'll be talking about later—the weapons that will enable you to improve your credit. In this chapter, that's exactly what you'll learn to do—read and understand your report.

It would be nice if all three of the CRAs could agree on a single format for presenting the information in these reports, but of course they can't. They are all in competition with each other, don't forget, and each company thinks it has the best method for laying out the data.

> Consequently, a report from Experian is going to look quite a bit different from a report from TransUnion or Equifax. I wish this wasn't true, but there it is.

In addition to individual reports from the various CRAs, you can get a "blended" report, which is basically a single report that summarizes the information gathered from all three CRAs. This is what you get from the source that I recommended in the preceding chapter, and there are other online companies that make blended reports available as well.

The good news is that even though the look, feel and organization differs from one CRA report to the next, and from individual reports to blended reports, they all have basically the same information and the same levels of detail.

So my goal here is to educate you to a point where you can read and understand any kind of report, regardless of where you got it. I'm going to cover the essential ingredients, the common elements that you'll find in all reports.

Your Identity, or Personal Information

Every report has detailed, personal information about you--your name (or names, if you have changed your name), your date of birth, your current and previous addresses, your employers, and of course, your Social Security Number (they have the entire SSN on file; but they usually just print out the last four digits for security reasons). This information is assembled when the credit reporting company first "discovers" you—when your first lender first reports your existence to the CRAs.

It's extremely important to review all this information for accuracy, but don't be alarmed if you discover variations in some of this data. It's normal to see your name with and without your middle initial or your middle name, and it's common to see past employers and past addresses listed on one report and not another. It's NOT OK though if you see your name seriously misspelled, or if you see bogus addresses or employers listed.

If you see errors of this kind, it's likely that there will be serious errors in your credit accounts due to sloppy reporting by the lenders, slap dash recording of the data by the CRAs, or both. Later we'll be covering in detail how to correct errors in your report.

Your Credit Accounts

This is the heart and soul of your report. This is where you'll find each and every one of your debts. With respect to each one, you'll see a great deal of information, including all or most of the following:

- The name and address of the creditor,

- The account number,

- The nature of the debt contract (whether it is a credit card, an installment loan, a real estate mortgage, or whatever),

- The most recent outstanding balance,

- The date you opened the account or signed the original contract,

- Whether the account is now open or closed,

- Whether you now are paying on the account as agreed (whether you are current with your payments),

- Whether you have ever been 30 days, 60 days, 90 days, or more than 180 days late with a payment and if so, exactly when you were late,

- Whether the original creditor has turned the account over to collections, and if it has, the name and address of the collection agency,

- Whether the account has been charged off (whether the lender has given up trying to collect and instead has elected to take a loss on the account—at least on paper),

- A month-by-month payment history, usually going back at least 12 months and sometimes much longer,

- If the account is revolving (like a credit card), the dollar amount of the credit limit,

- If the account is an installment loan, the original amount of the loan and the term of the loan (two years, five years, or whatever),

- Whether or not you are solely responsible for payment (responsibility could be joint, as it often is on car loans and mortgages, or you could have co-signed for someone).

This is the information that creditors continually update with their periodic reports to the CRAs, and it is this information that is so often not reported correctly or is not recorded or compiled correctly. If there are errors, it could be the fault of the original creditor, the credit reporting agency, or both. Regardless, you will learn to use these errors to your advantage.

> Don't be intimidated by the amount of information you find in this section of your report. In fact, I encourage you to think of it as your own personal land of opportunity.
>
> To the extent there are mistakes and errors in this "accounts" section, you'll be using them as weapons against the OCs, the CAs and the CRAs; and I'm going to teach you how to do it.

Your Public Information

For all the reasons that we've been discussing, lenders, employers and others are very interested in information directly related to your voluntary debt. They get this information when they want it by requesting it from the CRAs. As we've seen, it shows up in the "Credit Accounts" section of your report. You probably won't be surprised to learn that these same people (the lenders, employers, etc.) also want to know whether certain "involuntary" events have occurred in your life—events like bankruptcies, court judgments and tax liens.

When you file for bankruptcy, your filing becomes a public record in the bankruptcy court. If you are sued and the court hands down a judgment against you, the decree becomes a public record in that court. If the state or the IRS files a tax lien against you, that fact is recorded in the registry of deeds in the county where you reside. If you are ordered to pay child support, the order is kept on file with at least one state agency, and depending on the state, perhaps in local court or registry records as well.

All of these "public records" keepers—the courts, the deeds registries, and certain state and local authorities—regularly report certain kinds of filings to the three CRAs. The filings they report include the following:

- Bankruptcies,

- Court judgments,

- Foreclosures,

- State and federal tax liens,

- Child support payments orders.

If you have any of these events in your relatively recent past (usually within the past 7-10 years), this is where it shows up in your report.

Consumer Statement (Personal Statement)

This section might be designated your "Consumer Statement" or your "Personal Statement," depending on the source of your report. Regardless, if you're reading this book, then this section is almost certainly blank. It has no data in it because it is reserved for statements of dispute that you have filed with the CRA at some point in the past. If you're new to credit reports and have no history of trying to improve your credit, you won't have filed any disputes.

Under the FCRA, you have the right to file a written dispute about anything contained in your report. If you disagree with how a credit account is reported or if you want to make some other note on your report, you may do so by writing to the CRAs and asking them to include the statement. A potential creditor could read the statement when they pull your report.

The Summary

Depending on where you obtain a copy of your report, you might see a "Summary Section." It provides an all-in-one, high level look at all the information found in your report. Again, the three CRAs don't all summarize your information the same way, but if your report has a "Summary Section," it probably will contain:

- The total amount of your debt, with subtotals for all your mortgage debt, all your revolving accounts, all your installment loans, and all your other debt if you have any,

- The total number of open, closed, and delinquent accounts,

- Total amounts for open, closed, and delinquent accounts.

The reason for the breakdown into mortgage debt, revolving debt and installment debt is this: Creditors like to see a "healthy" mix of different kinds of debt, and this section lets them assess this issue very quickly.

Your Summary also might contain a list of any "negative" items in your report. A negative item is any instance in which you have been at least 30 days late on any credit account.

The purpose of this section is to enable a busy loan officer to just go to the "Summary" section, see if the loan applicant's credit is basically sound, and make a quick decision about whether it will be necessary to delve into the report in more detail.

Inquiries

If someone decides to take a look at a current copy of your credit report, the CRAs record the fact. The call it an "Inquiry"; and every time someone checks your credit, it can show up on your report.

> "Why would anyone care about who has checked my credit?" you might be asking yourself. Well, the reason your creditors care is simple: If you've got several recent inquiries on your report, this might mean that you're out trying to borrow more money than you will be able to repay. They see this as a danger signal.

In this "Inquiries" section, you see the identities of those who have requested credit information about you.

- You'll recognize some of them (like maybe the name of the bank that recently gave you a mortgage), because you agreed to let them check your credit.

- You might not recognize some of the others. The reason is that certain companies can request your credit without asking you first. A good example is the credit card company that sends you an offer for which you have been "pre-approved." They might have checked your credit before they sent you the offer.

Here's the significance of all this. Inquiries can lower your credit score, for the reason highlighted above. That's the bad news. The good news is that not all inquiries have this effect. Inquiries come in two flavors—hard and soft.

- **Hard Inquiries:** Your future lenders are really only interested in inquiries by other lenders that you authorize. For example, if you apply for a loan or a credit card, and in the process of applying you authorized the bank or credit card company to check your credit, that's a "hard" inquiry. It likely will have a marginal negative effect on your overall credit score. We'll have much more to say later about how your credit score is calculated.

- **Soft Inquiries:** Your future lenders don't much care about unauthorized inquiries. A good example of this kind of "soft" inquiry is one made by a credit card company that you have never heard of and have not applied to. These inquiries might show up on your report, but they don't have any effect on your score.

One more very important point, while we're on the subject of inquiries. When you request your own report and score, the CRA is aware of it of course, but they record the event as a soft inquiry. This is true whether you make the request directly to each individual CRA or use a third party online service to get your all-in-one report and scores (as I recommend). It doesn't hurt your score at all if you inquire into your own credit standing. You're not doing yourself any harm by pulling your report.

Well, that's it for your credit report for now. We'll have more on the subject later in the chapters to come, but let's move on to the other major component of your credit—your credit score. In the meantime, the following few pages are an example of a "dummy" all-in-one report.

Three-in-One
Sample Credit Report

Personal Information

Registration Information
Name: Clark S. Kent Address: 123 Main Street, Metropolis, NY 54321
Social Security Number: 001 23 4567

Identification Information

	Equifax	Experian	Transunion
	Reported	Reported	Reported
Name:	Clark Kent	Clarke Kent	Clark S Kent
Social Security Number:	001234567	001234567	001234567
Age or Date of Birth:	08/1966	08/1966	08/1966

Identification information is used to verify identity based on your social security number. It may reflect name changes or misspellings.

Address Information

	Equifax	Experian	Transunion
	Reported	Reported	Reported
Address:	123 Main St	123 Main St	123 Main St
	Boston, MA 54321	Boston, MA 54321	Boston, MA 54321
Date Reported:	03/1999	01/2002	10/1999
Previous Address	RR3	RR3	RR
	Dallas, TX 12345	Dallas, TX 12345	Dallas, TX 12345
Date Reported:	11/1998	12/2001	09/1999

Address information shows both current and previous reported mailing addresses

Address Information

	Equifax	Experian	Transunion
	Reported	Reported	Not Reported
Employer	Big Company, Inc	Big Company, Inc	
Address:			
Date Reported	02/1991	02/1991	

> Employment information identifies the current employer, as of the date reported.

Account Information

American Express

	Equifax	Experian	Transunion
	Reported	Reported	Reported
Account Type:	REVOLVING	REVOLVING	REVOLVING
Account Number:	00726	00726	00726
Payment Responsibility:	Individual	Individual	Individual
Date Opened:	03/1991	03/1991	03/1991
Balance Date:	04/2002	04/2002	04/2002
Balance Amount:	$704	$704	$704
Monthly Payment:	$21	$21	$21
Credit Limit:	$704	$6416	$704
High Balance:			
Account Status:	AS AGREED	CURR ACCT	Paid as agreed
Past Due Amount:	$0	$0	$0
Comments:	Charge	Charge	Charge

Bank of America

	Equifax	Experian	Transunion
	Reported	Reported	Reported
Account Type:	INSTALLMENT	INSTALLMENT	INSTALLMENT
Account Number:	001330	001330	001330
Payment Responsibility:	Joint	Joint	Joint
Date Opened:	12/1999	12/1999	12/1999
Balance Date:	05/2002	05/2002	05/2002
Balance Amount:	$351000	$351000	$351000
Monthly Payment:	$2972	$2972	$2972
Credit Limit:	$450000	$450000	$450000
High Balance:			
Account Status:	AS AGREED	CURR ACCT	Paid as agreed
Past Due Amount:	$0	$0	$0
Comments:	Closed Account		Closed Account

Account information reflects information reported by creditors, primarily credit card companies. Information includes:

- Type of Account (revolving, installment, etc.) Date Opened
- Balance
- Monthly payment
- Credit Limit
- High balance amount
- Past due amount
- Account status

Inquiries Information

Equifax

Name of Company	Date of Inquiry	Type of Business
Duke Electric	11/17/01	Unknown Credit Extension, Review, or Collection
CAPONEBANK	05/21/00	
CITIFINANCE	05/21/00	Unknown Credit Extension, Review, or Collection

Experian

Name of Company	Date of Inquiry	Type of Business
Duke Electric	11/17/01	Unknown Credit Extension, Review, or Collection
CAPONEBANK	02/15/01	

TransUnion

Name of Company	Date of Inquiry	Type of Business
Ford Credit	04/17/02	Unknown Credit Extension, Review, or Collection
BANK OF AMERICA	02/15/01	
INGUWAS	02/02/01	Unknown Credit Extension, Review, or Collection

> "Inquiries" provide a list of Companies that have "checked" the consumer's credit.

Collections Information

Texas GTE

	Equifax	Experian	TransUnion
	Reported	Reported	Reported
Collector:	TEXAS GTE	TEXAS GTE	TEXAS GTE
Account Number:	75930260	75930260	75930260
Date Opened:	06/1995	06/1995	06/1995
Balance Date:	09/2000	09/2000	09/2000
Balance Amount:	0	0	0
Date of Status:	09/2000	09/2000	**09/2000**
Status:	PAID	PAID	PAID

Sears Credit			
	Equifax	Experian	TransUnion
	Reported	Reported	Reported
Collector:	SEARS CREDIT	SEARS CREDIT	SEARS CREDIT
Account Number:	12812398912	12812398912	12812398912
Date Opened:	04/1994	04/1994	04/1994
Balance Date:	10/1999	10/1999	10/1999
Balance Amount:	0	0	0
Date of Status:	10/1999	10/1999	10/1999
Status:	PAID	PAID	PAID

Collection Activity Includes:

- The collecting company
- The account in question
- Date opened
- Balance date
- Balance amount (zero if paid)
- Date of Status (see below)
- Status

Public Records Information

Equifax						
Court	Plaintiff	Docket Number	Filing Date	Balance Amount	Account Status	Type
Rich County CT of NY			07/1998	$136767	Appealed	Tax Lien Federal
Hapsburg County CT of NY			07/1998	$240562	Appealed	Tax Lien Federal

Experian						
Court	Plaintiff	Docket Number	Filing Date	Balance Amount	Account Status	Type
Rich County CT of NY			07/1998	$136767	Appealed	Tax Lien Federal

TransUnion						
Court	Plaintiff	Docket Number	Filing Date	Balance Amount	Account Status	Type
No public records on file			07/1998	$136767	Appealed	Tax Lien Federal

> "Public Records" reflects information secured by the credit company from the court house, court records, and other public sources. It often includes tax liens, foreclosures, evictions, litigation, judgments,

Personal Information

None

> "Disputes" identifies consumer disputes of credit report information.

Consumer Statements

Equifax

You have no Consumer Statement on file.

Experian

You have no Consumer Statement on file.

TransUnion

You have no Consumer Statement on file.

> "Consumer Statements" reflects information provided by the consumer regarding credit claims and information.

Chapter 5:
UNDERSTANDING YOUR CREDIT SCORE

Some Questions and Answers

How did "credit scores" come about? Whose great idea was this, anyway?

To give you some notion of how credit scores came into being, let me ask you some questions. Let's assume you have a complicated, unpleasant, costly task that you don't like doing; but the fact that it's a pain, that it's slow, and that it costs a ton of money doesn't mean that you can ignore it--you still have to do it several times every day.

- Would you rather accomplish the task much more quickly?

- Would you rather the task was simpler and easier to understand?

- Would you like it if the task could be done for far less money?

Easy answers: Yes to all three questions, right? Of course. Now imagine that you're a lender who gets twelve loan requests every day. You could just grant all twelve loans, regardless of who the applicants are; but this would be a really bad idea. Some of them wouldn't pay, and you'd lose money. You don't want that (you really, really hate it when you lose money).

So--this means that you have to pull twelve credit reports each day to get some idea of who these applicants are and whether they're likely to pay you back. You have to decipher all the information in each report (and there's a lot there) before you decide whether you should make each loan.

The reports are complicated, and hard to understand, so you have several credit evaluation specialists on hand who are trained to do this for you. They work for you (unfortunately), and this means you have to supervise them and pay them. You don't like anything about this. The credit analysts are expensive, and they seem to take forever. They're a bottleneck in your loan approval process.

For years, this is how it was. As we've already seen, a modern credit report can be confusing, and in the early days of these reports they were much more so. Lenders would have to decipher the information themselves, and they had to hire experts to do it. Not just anyone had the training and experience to evaluate these reports. The process of dealing with them was cumbersome, expensive, and slow. The situation was ripe for a solution—something that would streamline the process and make it fast, simple, and much less expensive.

> As so often happens when rich, powerful interests have a problem that needs solving, someone steps in to provide the answer and make a pile of money in the process.
>
> Does anyone see a pattern developing here?

Enter Bill Fair and Earl Isaac. In 1956 these two gentlemen (an engineer and a mathematician) got together and formed Fair, Isaac and Company (FICO). They soon came up with a scoring system for assessing the creditworthiness of loan applicants. Eventually they developed a very sophisticated piece of "modeling" software that was designed to simplify the evaluation of credit reports and reduce the need for expensive credit analysts.

In concept, this credit scoring system (called the FICO System) is simple: A wide variety of information about consumers, like you and me, is fed into the FICO software program. This is the information that is contained in the credit reports. This program performs literally thousands of tests to compare your credit report data against that of everyone else. The results of these tests are converted into a points system to form a three digit "credit score". In reality, the system is not so simple of course (the mathematical algorithms are incredibly complex), and exactly how it works is proprietary (secret).

Simple or complex, and secret or not, it quickly caught on for these excellent reasons:

- It is very fast,

- It is inexpensive (at least compared to the cost of maintaining an army of credit review specialists),

- It is pretty reliable (banks and others quickly saw that the three-digit credit score did a pretty good job of predicting whether people were going to pay their debts on time or not.

In fact, the original Fair Isaacs software was so successful and popular that all three of the major CRAs (Equifax, Experian and TransUnion) decided that they had to have it. They all started using it to calculate scores. In turn, most of the CRAs' customers (the lenders, retailers, and creditors) soon "subscribed" to the software and began relying on the credit score to make their credit decisions.

These days, most of the credit decisions made in the US rely less on the detailed credit report and more on the three-digit credit score (the so-called FICO score).

On balance, the system is working pretty well for the lenders and the CRAs. It's working less well for borrowers. In fact, many consumer groups and public interest advocates have a lot of concerns and questions about the system, and with good reason: To the uninitiated (that's most of us), it can seem mysterious and confusing, and in general we just don't like having our entire life reduced to a three-digit number that we don't understand. Here are a few of the most common consumer questions and issues:

Question: What is the difference between a credit score and a credit report?

> **Answer:** A credit report is a detailed, complex summary and analysis of your spending habits, debt, and credit history. The Credit Score (FICO Score) is a three-digit number from 300 to 850 (higher is better) that's based on the information in your credit report and represents your relative "credit-worthiness" as a borrower.

Question: What is a "Good" credit score?

Answer: It depends on who's reading the score. The FICO System and the CRAs don't label a score as good or bad. They simply report the three-digit score to your lender. Each lender has an internal business process that defines good and bad scores for that lender. You might qualify for a good interest rate on a loan from Bank A, but Bank B might insist on a higher interest rate based on the same FICO score.

Here's how the American population stacks up in terms of scores:

- Thirteen percent of the population have a FICO of 800 and higher,
- Forty-five percent are in the 700-799 range,
- Twenty-seven percent have scores that fall between 600 and 699,
- Thirteen percent are in the 500 to 599 category, and
- Two percent have a score under 500.

In general, you will qualify for the best possible rates on most types of loans with a 750 or higher. A 720 will get you nearly the best rates. A 680 will get you a decent rate most of the time. Anything below a 600 and you will find it very hard to get any sort of loan at all. In the range from 600-680, you can probably find a loan or credit card, but the interest rate is going to be much higher than someone with a 720 would pay.

Question: Why is my credit score different at different lenders?

Answer: There are three reasons why your credit score might not be the same from one lender to the next.

1. Lender A might be getting its information from Equifax instead of Experian or TransUnion; Lender B might be relying only on TransUnion. Remember, it's voluntary for a lender to report to each bureau. Many won't report to all three, so each CRA might have slightly different

information about your history. For example, Experian might have information about your "late pay" on a car payment but TransUnion might not. If so, your FICO score from Experian will be lower than the one that TransUnion reports.

2. Though all three CRAs use the FICO process to calculate scores, each has tweaked the software a little to give slightly different weights to various factors. As a result, identical information can yield different scores, depending on exactly how the individual CRA has changed the math.

In addition, some lenders use factor weighting systems and mathematical calculations that they buy from independent companies other than Fair Isaacs. The scores that these systems yield can differ quite a bit from a CRA FICO score. Adding to the confusion is the common practice of generally referring to credit scores as "FICO" scores, even when the FICO software isn't used to calculate the score.

> This is all part of our national habit of adopting common names for things. It's what we do. We still commonly refer to all copiers as "Zerox machines," and for many of us, all facial tissue is "Kleenex." We're probably not going to change any time soon.

3. Finally, there is the fact that some lenders adjust the score after they receive it from the CRAs. This process isn't visible to you, but it happens; and it reflects differences in business approach and attitude from lender to lender. In practice, if your lender is uncomfortable with your type of employment, for example, it might "internally" reduce your score to address its concern.

Question: How do you know that your score is accurate?

Answer: You DON'T know, and that's a real problem. Your score is only as accurate as the data reported to the CRAs, and this data can be corrupted in several ways:

- **Mistake:** An item of information might be factually incorrect, or it might be inaccurately posted to your CRA file.

- **Timing:** There might be a delay between the date you do something (like pay off an account) and the date the information is reported to the CRAs and posted to your file.

- **Identity Theft:** Someone else might be creating activity under your name and identity.

Question: Can you check to see if your FICO score has been calculated accurately?

Answer: No, you can't. The scoring algorithms in the FICO system (and other scoring systems) are NOT public domain; they are confidential trade secrets. That means that there is no way for you to verify the accuracy of the calculations. In fact, you don't even know for sure what factors are considered in your credit score.

For example, if you have no credit cards at all, this has a negative effect on your score. If you have a great many credit cards, this too depresses your score. In order for your score to rise, the number of credit cards you have must be like Goldilocks' porridge: "not too hot, not too cold, but just right!" The problem is that consumers can't ever be sure what "just right" is. It's obvious that zero cards is too few and that 20 cards are too many; but nobody knows how many cards is ideal from the FICO score point of view.

The FICO model is often called "Black Box" software because you pump in information and a score pops out—there is no indication of what went into the calculations. This secrecy has generated a good deal of concern among consumer groups.

Over the last few years, under pressure, the scoring industry has implied, on several occasions, a willingness to provide more transparency. They have been reluctant, however, to follow through. They fear that widespread knowledge of the factors and the math they use will allow the consumer public to manipulate or "game" the system.

In summary, despite the issues and concerns surrounding its use, the FICO score is an increasingly important fact of your personal credit life. This is because the lenders and the CRAs like it—it's fast, inexpensive and from their point of view at least, reasonably reliable.

It isn't perfect, by a long shot, and exactly how it works is not public knowledge; but this doesn't mean we have to stay completely in the dark as consumers.

The Five "Credit Factors"

Fortunately, Fair Isaacs and the CRAs have shared enough information with the public to enable us to determine what the most important FICO factors are. There are five considerations, and each is weighed differently in calculating an individual score.

THE FIVE FICO FACTORS

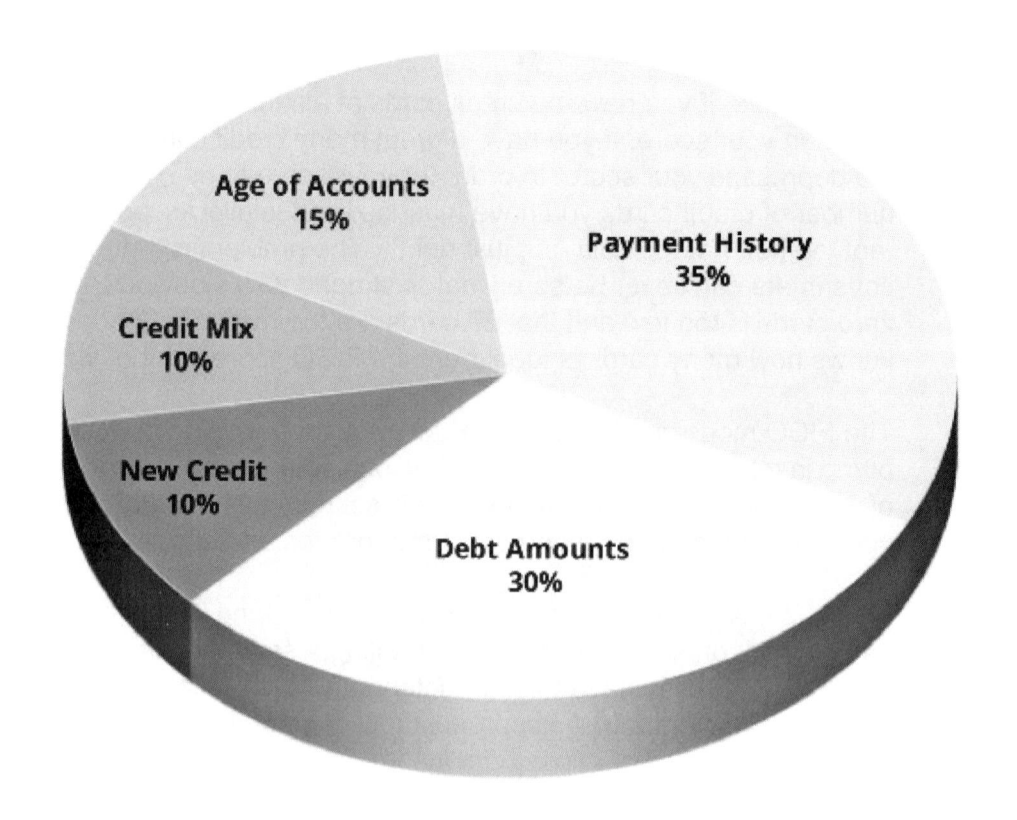

- Age of Accounts 15%
- Payment History 35%
- Credit Mix 10%
- New Credit 10%
- Debt Amounts 30%

As you can see from this pie chart, your payment history and the amount of your debt are by far the most important considerations. Next is the age of your accounts (how long you've had credit), followed by your credit mix (what kinds of credit you have) and how recently you obtained new credit.

What is your payment history (35%)?

It only makes sense that lenders would be most concerned about this factor, and weigh it more heavily than any other single consideration.

> Remember, the No. 1 article of faith of all lenders is this:
>
> "The best predictor of tomorrow's behavior is yesterday's behavior."

They believe that history dictates the future. In terms of their level of certainty, lenders put this principle right up there with "the earth is round," "night follows day," and "doughnuts are delicious."

If you're a borrower with a poor payment history, and you're looking for a new loan, you're going to have to overcome this prejudice. Now of course you'll argue that things have changed, that you've "turned over a new leaf," and that from now on you'll do better. Depending on your own personal story and how persuasive you are, your lender might believe you (it will help if he's a blood relative); but it always will be a very difficult sell. For the most part, lenders just can't get past the idea that if you haven't paid your debts in the past, you probably won't start now.

If you have a payment problem in your credit records, the severity of the impact on your credit score will depend on three considerations:

1. How long ago was the problem? The more recent the problem (say a "late pay"), the greater the impact on your score. As time passes, the impact will diminish. Again, this makes sense from the lender's point of view. If the cause of your problem is recent, it probably has not had time to go away. If your problem was in the distant past and you've paid on time in recent months, it's more likely that the cause of the trouble has disappeared.

2. How often did the problem occur? The more often the problem occurs, the greater the impact. Not shocking. No surprise here. The longer a poor payment history lasts, the more likely it is that it's a "habit." Habits are hard to break.

3. How serious was the problem? Obviously, the more serious the problem, the greater the impact on your credit score. For example, a payment that is 90 days past due will cause a bigger "hit" to your credit score than a payment that is 30 days past due. If your "90-day" is on your $2,000 monthly mortgage payment, this will lower your score much more than if you ignored a $27 minimum payment on one of your credit cards.

Among the payment history problems that are considered very serious, and that can drag a score down severely, are foreclosures, bankruptcies and court judgments.

How much of your available credit do you use (30%)?

This factor is also known as your "utilization rate." To understand why this factor works the way it does, again you have to put yourself in the position of a lender. Lenders want to know about the character of the person they're dealing with--whether the loan applicant is "responsible," especially with it comes to managing money.

A good way to measure this (they believe) is to look at how much money a person could borrow if they wanted to, and then look at how much of that total the person has actually borrowed. They reason that if you have a proven ability to resist temptation (not to get too moral about it), you're probably responsible with money. You'll probably pay them what you owe them and you'll probably do it on time.

They also consider that when people find themselves in tough financial circumstances, a common reaction is to start "living off the cards." They see high balances as a sign that something bad might have happened to your financial condition—an illness or a layoff, for example. Needless to say, they view this with alarm.

So, they look at the limits on your revolving debt (your credit cards, your store charge accounts). If they see that you have a card with a $5,000 limit, and that you usually run a balance of around $1,000, they like that.

They consider this a good sign. If they see that you often "max out" your limit on the card, they don't like that at all. They don't like it even if you routinely pay your big balance down to zero every month.

Here's how this works in practice: Let's say Mary owes $5,000 on a $15,000 account. John owes $2,400 on a $2,500 account. John will likely take a bigger hit to his credit score than Mary will, even though her debt is more than twice as large. In the eyes of the FICO software, Mary is a better, more responsible money manager than John.

> Now, I know that many consumers pay off their cards every month. Maybe you do too. This might be good debt management, but there are two reasons why it probably won't help your score much:
>
> 1. Credit card companies only report to the CRAs periodically. They report the balance that exists on the date of reporting. If you run a high balance before you pay off once per month, that high balance is the number reported.
>
> 2. The companies report the "high water mark" on your accounts, as well as the payment history.

Finally, it might be tempting to think that if you have three cards with limits of $5,000 each, it would be safe to run a high balance on only one of them and use the other two very little. Not so. For reasons not clear to me, the system will penalize your score for the high balance on the first card, and reward you little, if at all, for your sparing use of the other two cards.

If you want to have this factor weigh in your favor, you'll need to maintain low balances on all of your revolving credit accounts. Ideally, the balance on any card should never exceed 30% of the credit limit on that account.

How long have you had credit (15%)?

This is another "common sense" factor (unlike the one we just discussed). If you've had good credit for 25 years, you're more likely to maintain that level of performance than someone who has only a two-year credit history. The FICO software considers the following: The age of your oldest account, and the average age of all your accounts.

There are two lessons here.

1. If you're a young consumer who wants to qualify for the best rate when the happy day comes to buy a home, act now. Establish a good, positive account history as early as possible.

2. If you have some good older accounts, and a good score, think twice about opening a new account. The new account will reduce the average age of all your accounts, and possibly lower your score. It also might be prudent to close one or two newer accounts, if you can do it without inconvenience, to boost the average open account age.

When did you last apply for credit (10%)?

The impact of this factor is relatively minor, compared to those like your payment history and your account limits, but it is directly under your control and therefore deserves some attention.

Generally speaking, your score can be downgraded slightly if you open a number of new accounts within a short period of time. The FICO software weighs:

- The length of time that has passed since you applied for a new account.

- The length of time that has passed since you actually opened a new account,

- The number of new accounts you've opened, and

- The number of new accounts you've opened recently.

The bottom line is that creditors don't like lots of new borrowing activity. They're suspicious of it because they see it as a sign of irresponsibility and poor money management skills. The key word here is "new." As your new accounts become older accounts, and build up good payment histories, it becomes clear that you knew what you were doing all along, and the lenders become less concerned. That's why the "newness" factor counts the way it does and fades with time.

Of course, now and then you might need to open a new account (after all, once upon a time, all of your accounts were new); but it's in your interest to keep in mind that when you do it, the marginal effect on your score can be negative. Consider carefully before signing and submitting that next account application.

What types of credit do you have (10%)?

Another borrower characteristic that lenders like is a history of using more than one type of credit. They don't weigh a mix of loan types as heavily as some of the other factors, but they still like it—probably for a couple of reasons:

1. They know that certain types of loans, like real estate mortgage loans and car loans, require a much bigger financial commitment on the part of the borrower, and usually they involve some pretty substantial payments.

2. They know that mortgage and car loan lenders tend to delve pretty deeply into your employment and personal history, and if you survived the process, that's good.

3. They recognize that certain bank credit cards, like VISA, MasterCard, and American Express have more rigorous acceptance standards that some other kinds of local or regional revolving accounts. To the extent that you have these "stronger" accounts in your mix, that's good too.

On the whole, a good mix of credit includes a mortgage, an installment loan and two or three revolving (credit card) accounts.

Section III:
WHAT YOU CAN DO TO IMPROVE YOUR CREDIT, STARTING NOW

Chapter 6:
STEPS TO RAISE YOUR SCORE

In the previous chapter, we examined the five credit factors that significantly affect your credit score. In this chapter we are going to look at these same five factors, but now we're going to go beyond discussing what they are. Now we're going to focus on certain steps that you can take, or missteps that you can avoid taking, that will

- Cause your credit score to go up,
- Prevent your credit score from going down, or
- Both.

The following are nuts and bolts "Dos" and "Don'ts"—action items that you can use to start improving your financial life right now. I'm going to group them under the individual credit factors that they affect, and from time to time I'll refer back to the pie chart in the previous chapter.

Step 1—Manage Your Payment History

As we've already established, your credit payment history (the biggest slice of the pie chart) counts for about 35% of your credit score; so making sure you do everything you possibly can to establish, maintain, or improve your own personal history is huge for you. If you've resolved to turn a page in your life and start doing things differently when it comes to your bills (and if you're reading this book, that's exactly what you've done), then this is the place to start.

The FICO algorithm (the software, the math, the calculator—whatever you want to call it) takes three things into account when evaluating this factor:

1. How often have you failed to pay on time?
2. How far "past due" were you?
3. How much did you fail to pay?

Here are some action items that will help you (some are obvious; others, not so much):

- Pay everything on or before the "due date" if you can.

- Use an automatic payment system for loans with fixed payments (installment loans, mortgages, etc.); and for revolving credit payments establish a reliable calendar or "reminder" system that you can count on.

- Never "skip" a payment. Even if you can't pay a bill on the due date, don't just let it go for a month. Creditors normally don't report a "late pay" to the CRAs until an account is 30 days past due, but there is no guarantee that they won't. If you find that you can't pay a bill until it is 10 or 20 days late, make the payment as soon as possible. Above all, don't let the account go unpaid for 30 days.

- If you're "short" in a given month and you can't pay all your bills, do whatever you have to do to come up with the necessary money. Borrow it from a friend, draw down on your savings if you have any, sell something of value on eBay, hock your guitar, whatever; just don't let any of your creditors report that you are "late" on any of your accounts.

- If all else fails, and you're facing the prospect of two late pays in a single month because you can't quite get the money together to pay them both, then pool what you have available and pay one of them. Two late pays is much worse than one.

- If your minimum payment is $50 and you only have $25, don't just send in the $25 and call it good. This will register with your lender as a missed payment, and after 30 days it will likely be reported as a "late pay." Instead, wait a few days if you must, find the additional $25 and send in the $50 payment as soon as possible.

- If your financial life is in a bumpy stage (maybe you're facing reduced hours at work, or more expenses than normal) take stock of your revolving credit. If you have several cards, they're all going to require minimum monthly payments. If it looks like you might have trouble meeting the "minimum monthlies," consider transferring some balances as necessary to pay one or more down to zero. This will reduce the chances that you'll end up later with a "30-day" on your record.

There's one more consideration that doesn't necessarily affect your credit score, but it's still very important. If you're only a few days late on a credit card, the lender probably won't report a "late pay," but a "late pay" isn't the only bad thing that can happen. Depending on the terms of your credit card contract, the lender might be entitled to raise your interest rate on the card if you're late only a few days. You want to avoid this result whenever you can.

Step 2—Control Your Use of Available Credit

Approximately 30 percent of your credit score is calculated by weighing how much of your available credit you actually use (see the 30-percent slice in the pie chart). It's almost as important as your payment history. The scoring system's main concern is how you are handling your revolving credit (your credit cards). It looks at how much you owe on your cards and compares that amount to the credit limits on those cards.

The closer you get to your limits on your cards, the lower your credit score will be. If you want to have this factor weighed strongly in your favor, here are the measures you need to take:

- Make sure you know the credit limits on all your cards, and don't let the balance on any of your cards climb above 30 percent of the limit. For example, if the limit on one of your cards is $1,000, don't let the balance get above $300.

- If you have a number of cards, but you have a favorite that you like to use and you often run a balance near the limit, stop doing this. Instead, spread your monthly card use among your various cards, keeping the balance low on each. Figure out a system that works for you—For example, if you have three cards with comparable limits, use one card for the first ten days in the month, switch to another for the next ten days, and so on.

- Whether or not you pay the entire balance on your cards every month, send in your payment as soon as possible. This will increase the number of days each month that your account shows a low balance, and this in turn increases the likelihood that this low balance will be the number that your card company reports to the CRAs.

- If you have a card that doesn't have a preset limit (like American Express), the credit card company reports the highest balance that you have established since you got the card, and the CRAs treat that high balance just like a credit limit for purposes of calculating your utilization rate. If you have such a card, figure out what your historical high water mark is, and don't let your future balance climb above 30 percent of that amount.

> If you look back in your statements and you see that your highest balance was pretty low (maybe you've always used this card sparingly), then transfer some balances from other cards to this account to pump up the balance, pay the card down to zero right away, and then go forward from there reverting back to your usual light use of the card.

- If one of your cards is above 30 percent and you have other cards that are not, don't be afraid to transfer balances as necessary to get all the utilization rates below 30.

- If you don't have the cash flow to get all your cards below 30 percent and keep them there, go through the exercise of spreading everything out and getting as close to 30 percent on each card as you can. For purposes of helping your score, a 40-percent utilization rate is better than a 70- or 80-percent rate.

- If you have a card with a high limit (say, $20,000) and your other cards have lower limits (maybe $5,000 each), do what you have to do to get the $20,000 card's utilization rate down to where it should be. Do this even if it means that you'll go over 30 percent on one or more of your other cards. A high utilization rate on a card with a high limit hurts your score more than a 30-percent violation on a lower-limit card.

- If all else fails, don't be afraid to call your credit card company and request a limit increase. Be sure to talk with them first about exactly how to do this and whether you'll likely qualify for the increase you're looking for.

You also might ask if they intend to pull your credit report as part of the process of deciding whether to grant your request for an increased limit. If you're only talking about one card, you're trying to get your 35-percent utilization rate on that card down below 30, and you've had a number or recent "inquiries," then the cost of another inquiry on your record might not be worth it.

- Don't assume that you can run a high balance, pay it off at the end of the billing period, and by so doing escape the "utilization rate" trap. You probably won't. Credit card companies report the balance that shows on your account on the date they send in their report to the CRAs. You might get lucky--they might report on the very day your full-balance payment is posted and your balance goes to zero—but it isn't likely. Chances are they'll decide to send in the report on your account when the balance is way above 30 percent of the limit.

- Don't assume that you'll be OK if you have an overall utilization rate of under 30 percent for the combined limits on all your cards. You won't. It's the utilization rate on each individual card that counts.

- Finally, if you have only one or two revolving accounts and you're running above 30 percent on either or both, consider opening another account or two. As you'll see in the next section, opening a new account isn't always a good idea from a scoring point of view, but the positive effect of getting your cards below 30 percent should outweigh any negative effect resulting from a new account.

Step 3—Age Your Accounts

How long your various accounts have been open counts for about 15 percent of your total FICO score. The scoring system weighs two considerations:

1. How old is your oldest account?

2. What is the average age of all your accounts?

The older your accounts are, the better the system likes it. Here's what you can do to manage this issue:

- Open credit accounts as early in your adult life as you can. Assuming you handle them like you should, they'll just sit there in your report and build credit score strength for you over the years. When it comes time to make a big purchase, like a home, your older accounts might make the difference in qualifying you for a lower rate. Remember Jack and Jim and the frightening amount of extra money that Jim's mortgage cost him over the years.

- If you have plenty of credit, and you have some new accounts that you're not using, close them. This will bump up the average age of your remaining older accounts.

- Don't open new accounts without a good reason. The next time you hear a store clerk offer to take 40 percent off the purchase price if you open a store account then and there, politely decline. If you don't, that new credit line will show up on your credit report, and the negative impact on your score will probably cost your far more in the long run than any savings you might enjoy on today's store purchase.

- Of course, from time to time you'll have to open a new account; but try to do it when you're not contemplating a major credit purchase (like a home or a new car). If you can put some months or years between your last new account and your application for a big installment loan, this will help you. The "new" account will have become "older," your credit score will be higher, and the rate on that home or car loan will be lower.

Step 4—Mix Your Credit Types

The credit scoring system looks favorably on variety, and as we saw on the pie chart, "credit mix" weighs in at 10 percent. Your score will be marginally higher if you have more than one type of credit. What do I mean by "type"?

Well, one basic type is the installment loan, which is a loan on which the amount owed is fixed at the beginning of the loan, and fixed monthly payments consisting of principal and interest (installments) are required over the life of the contract. This type of loan comes in two flavors: secured and unsecured (signature).

1. A secured installment loan involves collateral—something that you agree the lender will have the right to take away from you and sell if you fail to pay the loan as agreed. The most common examples are car loans and real estate home mortgage loans.

2. An unsecured loan does not involve any collateral. In essence, the lender agrees to make the loan on the strength of your signature (thus the name, "signature" loan). A good example of an unsecured loan is a student loan.

Whether they are secured or not, installment loans have a predetermined life span. If you make your payments on time over the life of the loan, the contract is paid off and the account relationship ends. For example, if you finance your car for five years and at the end of the period you pay off the note, you own the car free and clear and the account is closed.

The other basic type of personal credit is the revolving account. Credit cards fall into this basket, along with various kinds of store charge cards. The amount of the outstanding balance is NOT fixed at the beginning of the contract, and neither is the amount of the monthly payment that will be due. You can borrow, pay back, borrow some more, pay back, and on and on. This can go on indefinitely, month after month and year after year. That's why it's called a "revolving" account.

Finally, there is a common loan type that is a kind of hybrid—a combination of both an installment loan and a revolving credit account. What I'm talking about here is the home equity loan. It has features of both basic types. With most home equity loans, you can borrow, pay back and borrow some more (just as with a credit card), but it is secured by your home just like a normal real estate mortgage. If you don't pay, the bank can foreclose on your house (very unlike a credit card).

The scoring system likes to see a mix among these various types. Here are some guidelines and things you can do to help yourself and your score:

- Try to have some installment loans, but not too many. Probably two or three is best from a credit scoring perspective. Probably at least one of them should be secured.

- If you don't have any installment loans at all, consider simply borrowing some money from your bank on a signature note (say, $5,000), and deposit all of that money in an interest-bearing account at that same bank. Leave it there and don't touch it.

  Arrange to have the monthly payments on your new loan paid automatically from your new deposit account. To some extent the interest on the deposit account will offset the interest on the loan, and in the end the loan will only cost you a few dollars. Your score will benefit because you will have paid back a secured installment loan—always a good fact to have in your credit file.

- If you don't want to put the loan proceeds in a bank account, you can still establish a secured installment loan. If you own something of substantial value (maybe a car that you intend to drive for awhile and that you own free and clear), then offer it as collateral on your new loan. Make the term short, pay it off as agreed, and help out your credit score.

- Have at least three revolving accounts, in addition to your installment loans, and don't limit yourself to local or regional store charge cards. Accounts with national companies, like American Express, VISA and MasterCard, will improve your score more than accounts with local merchants.

Step 5—Minimize New Credit

This last factor counts for the final 10 percent of your credit score. It's similar to the factor that weighs the ages of your accounts, but lenders have a very different reason for being interested in this "new credit" issue.

- They care about account ages because the longer you have been making timely payments on your accounts, the more likely it is that you will keep up this behavior.

- They care about this last factor, new credit, because if you have very recently applied for additional credit, it's more likely that you have reached the edge of your ability to handle all your monthly obligations (or that you're getting closer to the edge).

Of course, once you establish your ability to handle your new account over a period of a few months, it becomes obvious that you weren't at the edge after all, and the concerns lessen.

Here are the considerations that the scoring model takes into account:

- The length of time that has passed since you applied for a new account,

- The length of time that has passed since you actually opened a new account, and

- The number of new accounts you have opened recently

Here are a couple of tips for dealing with this last factor:

- You should open accounts early in life and keep them open if you can.

- Don't let vendors check your credit unless you are serious about a purchase. The CRAs see this as a new credit application and count it against you.

- Finally, you should be guided by the same considerations that I detailed for you in the discussion of Factor 3. They all apply with equal force here.

Chapter 7:
HOW TO REMOVE NEGATIVE ITEMS FROM YOUR REPORT

In the previous chapter, I went into a lot of detail about how you can organize an d conduct your financial life in ways that will improve your credit rating over time. All of my recommendations will help you, and I urge you to follow them because I know that if you do, you'll upgrade your report and raise your score.

But for the most part, the measures we've talked about so far won't have the effect of removing negative items from your report. By "negative items" I mean certain unfavorable entries that are in your records right now—marks against you that are given negative weight in the scoring process. These adverse entries are killing your FICO score.

> Remember that your FICO score is just a mathematical reflection of the various facts that appear in your credit report. That's all it is. This means two things:
>
> 1. Every negative fact in your report drives your score down, and
>
> 2. If a negative fact disappears from your report, your score goes up.

Unless you already have a terrific credit score (in which case you must be reading this book out of idle curiosity), you almost certainly have some negative marks in your report right now. Needless to say, you want to make these adverse entries go away if possible. I'm here to tell you that it is more than just possible: You can get rid of some (or all) of the negative items in your report and dramatically improve your score in short order. In this chapter, I'm going to show you exactly how to do it.

How am I going to do this? Exactly how is this going to work? Well let me assure you, first of all, that I'm never going to suggest that you do anything improper or dishonest, or that you say anything to anyone that isn't true. That would be wrong, it's completely unnecessary, and we're not going to go there. In fact, I'm going to show you how to clean up your report by using three simple (and completely legitimate) tools:

1. Polite requests for favors,

2. Written requests for information, and

3. Written demands for action.

These tools work because they rely on (and make use of) various provisions of the three federal laws that we discussed earlier in this book:

- **The Fair Credit Billing Act (FCBA):** This law targets your lenders (your OCs). It requires them to bill you fairly, accurately and completely. It affords you certain rights, including the right to dispute your bills.

- **The Fair Debt Collection Practices Act (FDCPA):** This statute regulates the collection agencies (CAs). It spells out what debt collectors can and can't do, it outlaws many abusive practices that used to be common in the industry, and it dictates what CAs must do when they receive requests for information.

- **The Fair Credit Reporting Act (FCRA):** This law focuses on the credit reporting agencies (CRAs). From the perspective of getting negative items removed from your report, it's most important feature is that it prescribes exactly what a CRA must do when it receives notice that a report is being disputed.

What we're going to do in this last chapter is put these laws to work for you. We're going to place certain legal weapons in your hands—weapons made available to you by Congress—and show you how to use them.

> Don't worry: You're not going to have to wade through the details of these federal statutes. I'm going to highlight and explain the parts you need to understand.

Before we get started, please locate your credit reports and get them in front of you. If you haven't done so already, print out your reports in hard copy.

Identifying Your Negative Items

Your first order of business is to carefully comb through your reports and do two things:

1. Locate all the negative items, and

2. Categorize these negative items according to my system.

The reason we need to categorize the adverse marks is simple—we're going to need different tools to get rid of different types of negative items. You'll need something to write with for this project, and I suggest a red marker because it makes it easy to find your marks later. Once everything is identified and put into the proper baskets, we'll get started with the removal tactics.

Here are the steps you need to take right now to locate and categorized your negatives:

1. Go through all three reports (or your combined 3-in-1 report, if that's what you have in front of you) and locate all items where you paid late, but not more than 30 days late. Take your marker and write "GOODWILL" next to each of these items.

2. Go through all reports a second time and find any items listed as 60 days late. Next to these write "GOODWILL or FCBA."

3. Now make a final pass, and this time I want you to find any items that are anywhere from 90 to 150 days late, <u>but have not been sent to "collections" and have not entered "charged off" status.</u> Mark these items "FCBA."

4. Now look for items that have entered collections status. You'll see the word "collections" on the Experian and TransUnion reports; Equifax designates these items as "R9" in the status column.

    a. If the collections item is <u>unpaid</u>, and if it was reported to the CRA by a collection agency (CA), write the word "VALIDATION" next to it.

    b. If the item is <u>unpaid</u>, but was reported to the CRA by the original creditor (OC), write "INVESTIGATION" next to it.

    c. If the item is <u>paid</u>, write "INVESTIGATION" next to it, regardless of whether it was reported by a CA or an OC.

5. Finally, look for items indicating that they have been charged off. Equifax uses the code "I9" to designate these. If you have any charge offs, mark them "INVESTIGATION."

OK, that's it for now. Believe me, I understand that this doesn't make a lot of sense just yet; but the plan is starting to come together, and you truly are on your way to a higher credit score. Next I'll explain exactly how to deal with the items you identified in your first run through—those that you marked "GOODWILL."

Removing Items Marked 30-60 Days Late

As I'm sure you noticed as you categorized your negative items, we grouped them according to the level of seriousness (a 30-day late pay is not as big a problem as an account that is in collections). We did this for a reason—the more serious the negative item, the more potent the weapon needed to get it removed from your report.

For the least serious items (the 30-day and 60-day late pays), you can use something called a "goodwill letter." Its target is the original creditor (OC). It can be very effective if used correctly, and in the right circumstances.

> Let's say you've been a customer at Home Depot for many years, and got a Home Depot card a few years back to take advantage of a "No Payments/No Interest for 6 Months" offer.
>
> You paid on time for several years, but then you ran into some health problems that really got you off track. You missed a couple of regular payments.
>
> This was a couple of years ago. Since then, you've been paying on time, and you've always been a good, loyal customer.

This is the kind of situation that is made to order for the goodwill letter. The basic idea behind this device is simply to ask for forgiveness, to request a favor from the original creditor.

Of course, there's nothing to stop you from trying a goodwill letter in just about any situation involving an OC, but you'll have the best results if

- You were no more than 30 to 60 days past due,

- Your late pays came after a period of several months of timely payments, and

- You have established a good payment history of several months (preferably a year or more) after the last late payment.

The longer the period after the last late payment, the better you chance for success. The reason for this is that these letters work best when you can basically say: "Hey, I screwed up. It won't happen again. As you can see, I've been making my payments on time since the late payment. So please, would you mind cutting me a break just this one time?"

This works because the OC wants you to continue to make timely payments and to keep using its services or shopping at its retail store.

> It also works because you're dealing with real people on the other end. An actual living, breathing person is going to read your letter and make a decision about what to do; and people (as opposed to computers) respond well to a humble, polite approach.

There isn't any guarantee that writing a goodwill letter will work, of course; but they very often do, and it's easy to mail them out. There's no downside other than the cost of a stamp.

So what exactly should you put in your "goodwill letter"? To help you with that, I've put three sample goodwill letters in the appendix.

If you're in a real hurry, you can just use these as your own; but you'll have more luck if you write in your own words, using your own story. Remember, a goodwill letter is a genuine request for help; and you want to be sincere and write about your own unique situation if possible. The best letters will come from you, be uniquely written for your situation, and allow your personality to come through. Don't forget to

- Give a good reason why you had trouble during the time the payments were late, and explain why your situation is different now and why it won't happen again.

- Give a good reason why you are writing now. Maybe you're applying for a home loan, a car loan, etc.

- Don't be demanding or pushy with this request. That sort of attitude is better saved for other, heavier tactics that we will cover later. A goodwill letter should be genuine and forthright, and have a humble tone.

- It's helpful if you can mention that you've been a loyal customer and intend to be a customer for many years to come. Remember, they want to keep you as a customer.

- Make sure you take responsibility for the late payment. Let them know that you realize you should have been more careful. Don't try to blame everything on your situation at the time.

Another note of Caution: Before you start sending off goodwill letters, you need to make sure of one thing first—namely that the late payment you're writing about is actually showing on your credit report. It's not enough that you know a payment was late. It has to be showing up on your report. Sometimes a creditor might not report a late payment at all, and if that's the case with your late payment, so much the better. No harm; no foul. Let it go. The last thing you want to do is send them a reminder or jog their memory.

Good luck with your goodwill letters. Go ahead and get a few done right now.

Removing Items Marked 90-150 Days Late

Now we're getting into the more serious negative items, and we're going to need more serious methods for dealing with them. If the goodwill letters were "softball," the tactics I'm going to describe from here on out are "hardball."

Again this doesn't mean that you're going to be unpleasant, contentious, or intimidating. It just means that you're going to make express use of your legal rights.

Trying to intimidate OCs, CAs and CRAs would be a complete waste of time and effort. The main reason these tactics work isn't because these companies are afraid of you. They're not. They just see you as an irritation. They want you to go away.

> You're going to be asking for information that they don't want to provide. You're going to be demanding action on their part that they don't want to take. Providing information and taking action always costs time, effort and money. By making these legal requests, you're giving them two choices:
>
> 1. Provide the information or take the actions that the law requires, or
>
> 2. Remove the negative item and thereby avoid having to do any of the things you're requesting.
>
> These tactics work because you basically just offer them these choices and they take the easy way out.

Remember that all of these companies are private, for-profit businesses. They exist to make money. They like to do things that make them money; they hate doing anything that doesn't make them money. In particular, they really don't like to do anything they see as an expensive nuisance. In the paragraphs to follow, I'm going to show you how to become an expensive nuisance. You're going to learn how to give these companies two choices; and removing your negative item is always going to be the more attractive option.

Let's cover a method you can use with original creditors (OCs) when you have 60-day to 150-day late payments showing on your report, but the amounts are paid in full. It doesn't matter if the late payments were fairly recent or from many years back. As long as the accounts are now current and were never charged off or placed in collections, this method can be applied.

Once again, you're going to be writing to your OC, but this time you're not going to be asking for any favors. The nice, humble tone will be gone. This is not a goodwill letter. This time you're going to be a little more aggressive. The idea here is to offer your OC a choice to either

- Provide you with certain documentary information, or

- Notify the CRAs to remove the negative item from your report.

You're hoping, of course, that they choose the latter option. But will they? Yes, they might very well. Here's why: The FCBA requires creditors to bill correctly and completely. This means that they must be sure that

- The account was created at your request,

- Every item billed to the account was billed correctly,

- Every billing statement was created in a timely manner,

- Every billing statement was sent to the correct address,

- The creditor never ignored your change of address requests,

- The creditor never ignored disputed charges, and

- All interest charges and late fees were computed in accordance with federal law and with any laws specific to your home state.

The creditors know what they're supposed to do under this law. You're going to be sending them a letter that asks them to prove to you that they have done everything that the law requires. You're going to tell them that if they can't provide the proof requested, you expect them to see to the removal of the negative mark on your report. You're banking on the fact that assembling and providing the requested information will take time, effort and money, but removing your negative item will be easy and quick.

You're also presenting yourself as someone who might resort to a couple of additional options if you don't get your way—namely, you might sue them in court or you might ask the Federal Trade Commission (FTC) to get involved in your claim (the FTC is the federal agency that has jurisdiction over enforcement of the FCBA and certain other consumer rights laws).

> If you were to sue, or to file a complaint with the FTC, the lender would have to get its own legal counsel involved, and this would cost them even more time, effort and money.

It's important to note that you won't be expressly threatening to do either of these things (you should never threaten to take any action that you don't intend to take), but the letter will have a tone suggesting that you are the type of person who won't stop if they ignore your request.

I like to call this approach the "Creditor Confusion" tactic. The objective is to leave the creditor wondering just what, exactly, you have planned. You're not making it easy for them to figure out your intent. You want the creditor to basically run through these thoughts when your letter arrives:

- "If we provide the information requested, we'll have to do a lot of work.

- This person might take legal action if we ignore this letter.

- It would be simpler and quicker to just remove the negative item.

- That looks like the thing to do."

There's one other feature of this tactic that I want to call to your attention. You don't need to claim that there were any specific problems with the way the creditor handled your account. This is worth repeating. You don't need to claim that the creditor did anything wrong. You simply want to exercise your right to ask for the documentation that proves that the creditor did nothing wrong—that the creditor did not violate your rights.

It's perfectly legal to request the information, and there is no risk at all as long as the creditor has been paid in full. I've prepared a sample letter for you to use as a reference when writing your own letter. You'll find it in the Appendix.

Again, I strongly suggest that you write your letter in your own words. Just use the sample as a guide. You want to appear as a person who is knowledgeable about consumer rights. You don't want to look like someone who is just using a form letter as a tactic, with no real plans to follow through. Let your own personality shine through in the letter; it's more likely to have the desired effect.

Removing Collections Items That Remain Unpaid

There are some excellent tools available to help you get rid of collections items that you have not paid (and on which collection efforts are probably still ongoing), but before I discuss them with you I need to cover something extremely important.

Beware of the Statute of Limitations. Every state has a statute of limitations (an SOL) that applies to lawsuits brought to collect debts. They all work pretty much the same way.

> The language used in the individual state laws varies quite a bit in terms of style, but they all run along these lines: "All court actions to collect a debt must be filed within ____ years after the date the debt becomes delinquent, and not thereafter."

These statutes mean what they say. The practical effect is that once you stop paying on a debt, your creditor has a certain period of time (from one year to six years, depending on the state) in which to file suit in court. If the creditor fails to sue before the deadline, the court won't accept any filing after that, the case will be thrown out if it is brought, and the creditor is out of luck.

Once the deadline passes, the creditor no longer has any power to sue and enforce its claim in court. It can never, ever get a court judgment against you. This is huge! This is a good thing from the consumer's point of view.

Now, at this point in this discussion, you've probably got a couple of excellent questions:

1. Once the SOL has run (once the deadline passes) on my debt, does this mean that I don't owe the money?

2. Once the SOL has run, does it mean that the creditor must stop its efforts to collect?

The answer to both of these questions, unfortunately, is NO. You still technically owe the debt, and the creditor is still entitled to try to collect. What you creditor <u>cannot</u> do is haul you into court as part of its collection efforts.

Whether the SOL has run or not is always going to have a very important bearing on how you approach getting that unpaid collections item removed from your report. I encourage you to do your own research for the state you live in before attempting to deal with any of the unpaid collections accounts on your reports.

OK, so you know how long the SOL is, but how do you know when it starts? When does the clock start to tic? Unfortunately, the answer to this can be a little tricky. A good general answer is that the SOL starts to run (the clock starts ticking) once you've done something under the contract that would provide your creditor with a reason to sue you. Usually this "reason to sue you" is that you've failed to make a payment called for in the agreement--you are "past due" or "delinquent" on the account. But (and I can't caution you too strongly here) the triggering event can vary from state to state, and it can work differently depending on what the loan contract says. You should confirm exactly how it works in your state, with your loan, before you make a decision.

Why is all this talk about the SOL so important? Because you might not want to try getting an unpaid collections item removed from your report if the SOL has not run.

> Trying to get the item removed might end up being the equivalent of kicking a very big, very nasty, sleeping dog. It might prove to be just a terrible idea.

Yes, it's true that the unpaid collections item is a big negative on your report, but believe me; it's not taking nearly as big a bite out of your FICO score as a court judgment would. If your creditor has not yet sued you on the debt, and the SOL remains open, you run the risk of "reminding" the creditor that he should sue you.

This should not be a concern for you if the debt is small and you would be able to pay in full if your creditor sued. If that's the case, you know you're not running the risk of a judgment. If you can't pay, then you need to consider the risk.

- If the debt is really small (under $1,000), then it isn't likely that your creditor will go to the effort and expense of filing a lawsuit.

- If the debt is a little larger (say between $1,000 and $5,000), then depending on the availability of a small claims process in your state, your creditor might file against you.

- If it's more, you need to be very careful. If the debt is several thousand dollars or more, it becomes cost effective for the creditor to sue you.

-

These estimates are just my own personal opinion, and there are no bright lines on this issue. I recommend that you err on the side of caution. Bottom line: You want to avoid any further damage to your credit score and this means that you need to avoid a judgment at all costs.

Another thing to keep in mind is that after seven years, your unpaid collections item is going to disappear from your report if you do nothing at all. The FCRA says that it can't stay there longer than that. Regardless of the size of the debt, it isn't worth the risk of being sued if the item will soon be disappearing from your report of its own accord.

OK. That's enough about the SOL. Let's suppose you decide to try to get the unpaid collections item removed. How do you do it? You have a couple of options, depending on who placed the item on your report (whether it was a CA or an OC).

A CA Reported the Collections Item.

Most collections items are reported to CRAs by collection agencies (CAs). The CA is either trying to collect the debt for a client OC, or it has purchased the debt for a fraction of its original worth (in which case it's trying to collect some money on its own account). Either way, if a CA is involved in the collections item on your report, you have a very powerful weapon at your disposal called "debt validation."

The Fair Debt Collections Practices Act (which regulates CAs, remember) says that you have a right to ask a CA to "validate" any debt that it is trying to collect. If you make this request properly, and the CA can't validate the debt or they don't validate correctly, then they must remove the item from your report. This is a very powerful weapon.

When you use this tool, you're basically just asking the debt collector to prove to you that you actually owe what they say you owe, and that they (the CA) have a right to collect that debt. It just makes good sense that you should have this right. If you didn't, anyone could write you or call you up claiming that you owe them money. The validation process allows you to confirm that the debt collector actually has a real debt that belongs to you and that they have the legal authority to collect on it.

> A validation request is the equivalent of saying, "Hey, I never opened an account with you, and I don't know who you are. Please explain what this is in reference to and give me details about the alleged debt. If you can't provide this, please remove it from my credit report immediately."

You can request a validation at any time. This can result in a favorable response (deletion of the entry from your report) from a collection agency no matter when it's requested.

I've placed a good sample validation letter in the Appendix. Again, for reasons already discussed, you should write in your own words, using this letter only as a guide.

By the way, you'll notice that the sample letter requires that the CA communicate with you only in writing. There are two reasons for this.

1. CA telephone agents are trained to trip you up and get you to say or admit things that can hurt you. You don't want to give them this opportunity.

2. You want to establish a written record of exactly how the CA responds to your request, and when.

OK, you've sent out your letter. Now what? How do you know if what you get back in response is sufficient to meet the CA's legal responsibilities under the FDCPA? Well, on this issue, the FDCPA isn't very specific. It doesn't spell out exactly what qualifies as validation, so it's best to think about what a reasonable person would consider proof of the debt and the debt collector's right to collect. Good validation documentation might consist of some or all of the following:

- The original contract with your OC,

- Copies of bills the OC sent to you showing unpaid amounts,

- Demand letters from the OC addressed to you stating amounts owed,

- The contract by which the OC assigned the debt to the CA, or

- The contract by which the OC hired the CA to collect the debt.

Even if the FDCPA is a little fuzzy on what constitutes good validation documentation, it's pretty clear that one kind of response in particular WON'T fly. Your CA might try to sneak by with just sending you a printout from their database with some numbers on it that they claim is the "amount owed." This seriously will not work, and you should call them on it. If you get this response to your validation request, then you will need to write a more forceful letter.

This letter should

- State emphatically that you are not satisfied with the information received,

- Make it clear that you don't believe the information meets legal requirements,

- Demand that the account be validated with CURRENT records obtained from the original creditor,

- Restate your request for the name and address of the creditor to whom the money is supposedly owed,

- Restate your request for a copy of the contract showing that the CA has the authority to collect this debt, and

- Demand that if the CA can't provide proper validation of the debt it must remove the item from your credit report.

Along with this letter, you should enclose a copy of something called the "Wollman FTC Opinion Letter."

Remember that the FTC (the Federal Trade Commission) is the federal agency that is charged with administering the FDCPA, and it has jurisdiction over collections agencies. From time to time the FTC issues opinion letters, authored by lawyers on its staff, when it receives requests for clarification as to what the FDCPA actually means. It did exactly that back in 1993 when it heard from a gentleman named Wollman (who worked for a CRA). Mr. Wollman wanted to know whether a mere CA computer printout was enough to comply with the validation requirements of the FDCPA. The answer was a clear NO. I've included a copy of the opinion letter in the Appendix in case you need it.

These opinion letters don't have the force of law, but most people, including collections agencies and their lawyers, give them a lot of weight. Also, if you send along a copy of this letter it tells the CA in no uncertain terms that you are serious, and that you can't be taken lightly. Most people have no clue that these opinion letters even exist, and you'll be serving notice that you're not "most people."

When you go through the validation process, one of four things will happen:

1. The CA will remove the item,

2. It will validate and refuse to remove the item,

3. It will validate improperly, or

4. It will ignore you.

If the CA removes the item from your reports, that's first prize. Congratulations.

If the CA provides sufficient validation of the debt and refuses to remove the item, that's not good. If you can't pay the debt, the item will likely remain on your report until it hits the seven-year mark and is removed for that reason. If you have the ability to resolve the debt, you might want to think about doing so. Once the debt is paid, you can then try to get the item removed by writing directly to the CRA using the error dispute tactic.

If the CA either sends you insufficient documents or ignores you entirely, you have one more card to play. The FDCPA says that once a CA receives a validation request, it must stop any further "collection activity" until proper validation is made. Why does this matter? Because the FTC believes that continuing to report an adverse item to a CRA is "collection activity." The FDCPA doesn't say this explicitly (What else is new?), but the FTC issued an opinion in 1997 that does say it, and very clearly. I've included a copy of that letter in the Appendix.

If the negative item remains on your report after the CA has ignored you entirely, or has failed to respond properly to your second attempt at validation, then send them a copy of the Cass FTC Opinion Letter, along with a strong letter. It should say that

- Because they have failed properly to validate the debt and have not removed the item from your reports, they are in clear violation of the FDCPA,

- In light of their failure to validate, they are absolutely required to remove the item from your reports,

- You expect them to follow the law and remove the item immediately, and

- If they fail to remove the item, they are subject to legal action in court or investigation by the FTC.

Note that the words used in this last point are chosen very carefully. I'm assuming that when you write this letter, you won't have made the firm decision to either sue the CA or file a complaint with the FTC. If so, you can't say that you will sue or file a complaint if they don't behave (well, you can, but I don't recommend it). It's perfectly OK, however, to truthfully point out that the CA will be "subject to" such actions if they don't get with the program. This doesn't mean that you intend to take the actions; it only means that you could if you wanted to. Of course, if you have made the decision to sue or file an FTC complaint if the item isn't removed, you should say so. There is no reason to hang back from making the threat if you intend to carry it out.

The OC Reported the Collections Item.

Remember that I asked you to separate the collections items on your report into two groups—those reported by a CA and those reported by an OC. Here's the reason for that. You can't use the validation tactic if the OC reported the item. Validation gets its "juice" (its legal firepower) from the FDCPA, and that law applies to CAs, not OCs. This doesn't mean you're helpless to remove the item placed by the OC, it just means that you need to use a different tool.

Very shortly, I'm going to cover a method of disputing adverse items directly with the CRA. With that tactic, you write to the CRA and ask them to "investigate" the basis for the debt. You're basically asking for the same things you request in a validation letter; but you send the letter to the CRA instead of to a CA. I'll get into more detail on this in the material on removing errors from your report.

Removing Collections Items That Are Paid

If you have a collections item on your report that you have paid, there is good news and bad news.

- The good news is that now you don't have to worry about getting sued. No one is going to drag you into court or try to get a judgment against you on a debt that you've paid, no matter how long it took for you to pay it.

- The bad news is that you can't use the validation tactic to get the item removed. The FDCPA is pretty clear that validation is only available when the consumer disputes "the debt, or any portion thereof." If you've paid the debt, you've admitted the debt. It's gone, and the question whether you owed the money is resolved

This situation, like the unpaid collections item reported by the OC, is made to order for the "error removal" method, which is coming up shortly. For reasons that I'll explain when I cover report errors in detail, the fact that you've paid the debt can actually increase the likelihood of success in having it removed.

Removing Errors from Your Report

Now we've come to a tactic that is extremely powerful—the so-called Investigation Letter. This tool is used directly against the CRAs, and it draws its strength from the Fair Credit Reporting Act (FCRA). The FCRA is, compared to the FCBA and the FDCPA, a lengthy and tedious law (If you have trouble sleeping, you might want to print out a copy and leave it on your nightstand). Even so, it does a pretty good job of telling consumers what the CRAs must do once they receive written notice that a consumer disputes the accuracy of something contained in a credit report.

Here is the pertinent language of Section 611(a)(1)(A) of the law:

> "[I]f the completeness or accuracy of any item of information contained in a consumer's file at a consumer reporting agency is disputed by the consumer and the consumer notifies the agency, . . . the agency shall, free of charge, conduct a reasonable reinvestigation to determine whether the disputed information is inaccurate and record the current status of the disputed information, or delete the item from the file . . . before the end of the 30-day period beginning on the date on which the agency receives the notice of the dispute from the consumer . . . ."

It boils down to this: If you disagree with something in your report, you can require the CRA to investigate the accuracy of the item. If the CRA can't confirm the item's accuracy within 30 days, it must remove it. This is EXCELLENT.

It's important to understand that when you use this technique, you always need to be pointing to something about the entry that isn't quite right. This normally isn't a very tough obstacle to overcome. Here are a few examples of problems with an entry that might support an investigation request.

- A paid account might show a balance,
- The account number might be wrong,
- Your name might be incomplete or misspelled,
- You addresses, SSN, or other identifying information might be wrong,
- A stated balance might be wrong,
- A payment date or amount might be wrong,
- A late fee might be miscalculated or posted wrong,
- A "status" statement might be wrong (paid, unpaid, collections, charged off, whatever),
- A credit limit might be wrong,
- The date of last activity might be wrong,
- The creditor identification is not correct, or it is incomplete,
- A collections account might be listed twice,
- A payment listed as late might have been made on time (and not posted to the account on time),
- An account might not be yours.
- A judgment or a lien might not belong to you.

Are you going to be able to find an error in the entry you want to have deleted? It's very likely. Keep in mind that the CRAs are constantly compiling and updating millions of other records along with yours. The work is done largely by computers, or by people who might not be well paid or well trained—people who don't care about you at all. Conscientious attention to detail is in short supply; inattention, sloppiness and lack of care abound. The probability that there is something inaccurate about any given entry is very high.

As always, I'm supplying you with a sample letter and I've included it in the Appendix: Sample Investigation Request. Before you fire off your first request for an investigation, though, I have some recommendations for you about exactly how to use, and how not to use, this tactic.

- First, don't assume that you want to get rid of an item just because something about it is inaccurate. Credit report errors are not like people—they are not all created equal. Some errors are good, and you should leave these alone. For instance, if you have a good credit line that has never been late and it's somehow reported twice, it's most likely helping your score. Ignore it. If one of your credit cards is reporting a higher limit than you actually have, overlook it. It's helping your utilization ratio.

    Remember your purpose here: You're trying to help yourself, not your creditors or the CRAs. You're not required by any law to police the accuracy of your credit report, nor are you required by law to report errors. Your only concern here is to find ways to increase your credit score. If your credit report has inaccuracies that help you, so much the better.

- When you dispute inaccurate information with the credit bureaus, it's best to be as detailed and specific as possible. You should include

    - Your full name with suffix,
    - Your current address with proof such as a utility bill,
    - Any previous addresses from the last year,
    - Your date of birth,
    - Your SSN,
    - Your spouse's name if you're married,
    - A full description of the items you are disputing, along with a copy of your credit report and the items circled or highlighted,

- - An explanation of why the items are not correct, i.e. this is not my loan, CC, judgment, etc., and
  - A request that the CRA confirm the item through investigation or remove it.

- Don't dispute more than three or four items in any single letter. The law says that the CRA doesn't have to investigate if it "reasonably determines" that the consumer's request is "frivolous." What does that mean? Well, this is another one of those terms that isn't entirely clear, but you should assume that if you ask them to do too much work in any single letter, their reaction might be to just mark your request as "frivolous."

  True, they must tell you in writing if they decide your request is frivolous, and you'll have a chance to respond, but that's not a road you want to go down. Your objective here is to get the CRA to do what you want as soon as possible, not to aggravate them.

- Keep your tone courteous and professional. The more you "scream," the more likely you'll be seen as frivolous.

- Use Certified Mail Return Receipt for your letters. The 30-day clock starts to tick when the CRA gets your letter, so you want to be able to prove that date with your signed receipt. Keep a log or a calendar to record when you send your letters, and when you get back any responses.

- Make sure you send along with your dispute letter any proof you have that supports your position (a canceled check, a receipt of payment, relevant correspondence, etc.) The law says that the CRA is entitled to consider your request frivolous if you fail to "provide sufficient information to investigate the disputed [item]." The more detail and support you can offer, the less likely it is that this will happen to you.

OK, now that we've got all that out of the way, exactly what situations are appropriate for this "investigation" tactic? I recommend using it in the following circumstances:

- **When a "Collections" item has been paid.** It can be especially useful here because of how the investigation process actually works. When the CRA gets your request to "investigate," it sends off your request to the CA or the OC (along with all the info you've provided to support your request), and asks them to respond.

  The beauty of this situation is that if the debt has been paid, the CA or the OC has no incentive at all to even read through your request. Why should they? They've already got their money. At this stage they don't care whether the CRA removes your negative item or not. They were only interested in reporting the item as a means to intimidate you into paying. Now that you've satisfied the debt, their interest is zero.

- **When an unpaid "Collections" item was reported by the Original Creditor (OC).** Of course, if you have not paid, your original lender might be motivated to at least review the investigation request to see how much work is involved. The more tedious and labor intensive the request, the better, from your point of view. Regardless of the "hassle factor," there is a good chance the creditor won't respond. This is, after all, a debt that has gone uncollected for a long time.

- **When the item is a "Charge Off."** These negative marks are very serious. Like collections, they can do horrific damage to a credit score; so you want to get rid of them if you can. You can treat them just like "collections" as far as using this tactic goes.

  Don't forget about the SOL. If you haven't paid the debt, the request for investigation might result in a suit. You must weigh that concern, and take into account all the factors that I've already discussed. If the debt is large, or if it is really old, you might want to leave it alone for the reasons already covered.

Reinsertion:

OK, we're almost finished with CRA investigation requests, but there is one final aspect of this tactic that I want to make sure I cover with you. Even if you're successful in getting a negative item removed from your report, you should continue to monitor your reports to see if it reappears. It might. This is called "reinsertion" and it happens. Here's why:

The FCRA puts a very tight time-frame around this investigation process. The CRA must complete its investigation and respond to your request within only 30 days. That's not very long. It's not uncommon for them to send off your materials to the creditor or CA, hear nothing for 30 days, and then remove the item. Unfortunately, it might not end there.

If a week or two later the creditor sends the CRA proper validation documentation or corrects the inaccuracy, and certifies to the CRA in writing that the information supplied is complete and accurate, the item may be reinserted into your report.

In the event of reinsertion, the CRA is supposed to notify you in writing; but you shouldn't count on it. The item could just reappear. If it does, you can request to see the creditor's certification of accuracy and completeness, but this isn't likely to help you very much. You'll be better off challenging the accuracy and completeness of the item, as amended, and starting the process over again.

This "reinsertion" issue is just one more reason why, if you're serious about improving your credit and maintaining a good score, you should think about subscribing to a credit monitoring service (if not forever, then at least while you're working through the methods described in this book). It's easier and less expensive than having to pay for all three reports every few weeks.

Keeping Negative Items Off Your Report

I know that this part of the book is all about removing negative items from your report, but I would be remiss if I didn't cover how you can use "validation" to keep a black mark from ever showing up on your report in the first place.

When a debt is turned over to a collections agency, the CA is required by the FDCPA to notify you in writing that this has happened. This letter is called a "validation notice," and it bears this name because of what's in it. It must tell you

- How much money you owe,

- The name of the creditor to whom you owe the money, and

- That you have the right to request validation of the debt.

The CA must send you this letter within five days after an agent contacts you about the debt.

If you receive one of these notices, PLEASE, don't stick it in a drawer or put it on your "I'll-deal-with-this-later list." This is your chance to keep that collections item from ever reaching your report and hurting your score. Take it. This is the time for action.

Once the CA sends you the validation notice, it must wait 30 days before it can report to the CRAs that the item is in collections. If within this 30-day period the CA hears from you in writing that you are exercising your right to require validation, it can't report the item until it completes the investigation. If, as so often happens, it can't validate the debt, then the collections item should never show up on your report.

So, it's always going to be in your interest to write to the CA immediately using a validation letter specially designed for this situation. Once again, you'll find a sample in the Appendix. Sample Validation Request 2.

You probably already understand this, but let me be very clear: If you should happen to fail to send a validation request within 30 days from receiving a notice of the debt collection, that does not mean that you forfeit your right to ask for validation later on. This is explained in § 809(c) "The failure of a consumer to dispute the validity of a debt under this section may not be construed by any court as an admission of liability by the consumer."

The 30 day window is only important because it provides you an opportunity to keep the debt from ever appearing on your credit report at all.

Final Thoughts

Congratulations on working your way through this book and taking aggressive action to improve your financial life (and your life in general). As I said at the outset, not everyone has the commitment and tenacity to do what is necessary to make things better, and you've set yourself apart.

I wish I could reward you with the promise that each and every one of these tactics always works, but of course they don't. They do, however, very often produce the desired outcome; and if you are organized, persistent and determined, you'll see concrete benefits.

I can tell you from my own personal experience that before long your reports will improve, your score will rise, and your access to credit will become easier and less expensive. You'll have less financial stress in your life as a result, and this will make a big difference in how you feel and how you see the world. You'll be happier.

The outcome here is going to well worth your effort. You can do it. Good luck.

Appendix:
FORMS AND SAMPLES

Sample Goodwill Letter 1

Date: _____

Re: Name of Creditor: _____
    Acc. # _____

Dear Sir or Madam,

I opened this account with you back in 20xx, and it remains open today. I use it regularly, and I look forward to doing so for many years to come. Your service has always been excellent, and your very professional representatives have never failed to treat me with consideration and respect. I value my relationship with your company.

I'm writing to you today to ask a favor. Unfortunately, I had _____ late payments in 20xx, and this has had a negative effect on my credit rating. I hope you will consider making a goodwill adjustment in your reports to Experian, Equifax and TransUnion by removing any references to these late payments. In weighing my request, please consider these points:

1. Except for the blemish already noted, my payment history has been perfect. There were no problems before the late payments, and there have been none in the _____ months since.

2. At the time of the late payments, I was in the midst of (here state the reason for the problem, for example, a job change, an illness or a divorce). I don't offer this in justification, but only to show that the reason for my late payment was the kind of event that isn't likely to happen again.

3. As you know, a lower credit score increases the cost of credit. In assisting me to raise my score, you will be helping me and confirming what I already believe—that _____ is willing to go the extra mile for its customers.

In closing, I want to thank you for your exceptional service throughout our long relationship. Whenever I get the chance, I recommend your company to my friends, and I will continue to do so whether or not you are able to grant my request for the goodwill adjustment.

Thank you so much for your consideration. I look forward to hearing from you soon.

Sincerely,

Sample Goodwill Letter 2

Date: _____

Re: Name of Creditor: _____
     Acc. # _____

Dear Sir or Madam,

I opened this account with you back in 20xx. Unfortunately, due entirely to my own failure in managing this account, there is a $_____ negative trade line in my credit file. At the suggestion of your customer service representative, I am writing you today to ask you to remove it.

The negative trade line results from a period in my life when I was going through (here describe a chaotic life event such as a job change, an illness or a divorce). During this time I failed to make timely payments. I was inattentive and disorganized, and I accept full responsibility. This failure was no one's fault but mine. I soon "woke up," however, and since then I have worked very hard to learn and apply the rules of personal financial management. I maintain a budget, I keep good records, and I make sure all my payments are made on time. These efforts have paid off, my financial house is in order, and my payment history from _____ through the present has been excellent.

I want to thank you for allowing me to maintain this account, in spite of my period of poor performance, and for giving me a chance to rehabilitate my creditworthiness. I am determined to make that second chance count.

Unfortunately, the negative trade line mentioned above is still in my credit file. If it remains, it will have serious consequences for me. I am currently shopping for a mortgage, and of course the existence of this trade line means that I won't qualify for the most competitive interest rates. Over time I will have to pay out additional interest that I can ill afford.

I know that the trade line only exists because of my own irresponsibility, but I believe that it no longer reflects my account performance. I hope you agree. I respectfully ask that you remove the negative trade line from your reports. A goodwill adjustment would be an enormous help to me, and it would demonstrate, once again, that you are willing to take a customer's personal circumstances into account in making credit decisions.

Whether you are able to grant this request or not, I will continue to be a loyal customer. I very much appreciate all you have done for me to date, and I want to thank you once again for your consideration. I look forward to hearing from you soon.

Sincerely,

_____

Sample Goodwill Letter 3

Date: _____

Re: Name of Creditor: _____
     Acc. # _____

Dear Sir or Madam,

I opened this account with you back in 20xx. I am writing you today to ask you to make a goodwill adjustment in your reports to Experian, Equifax and TransUnion.

I am well aware that I have not been careful in handling this account, and that any problems with the account have been my fault entirely. I should have been more aware of the status, and I should have known all along about the unpaid balance. Unfortunately, I didn't. I only became aware of it when it showed up on a credit report in _____ of 20xx.

Once I learned about the unpaid debt, I contacted you right away and paid it in full. I hope you can see that I did not willingly ignore my obligation. It's true that I did not give this account the attention it deserved, but I never intended to violate my agreement with you. I hope, and I respectfully request, that you will help me now by removing this blemish from my credit file.

I know very well that you have no obligation to grant my request, but I believe it is within your power to do so. I'm asking for a favor here—a goodwill gesture, a courtesy. As I understand the Fair Credit Reporting Act, you must make sure that the entries in your report are accurate, and that you have already done. The Act does not, however, require that every single transaction must appear in the record. I believe you have some discretion in deciding what is, or is not, in your reports. My purpose in writing today is to ask you to exercise that discretion in my favor and remove the negative reference from your reports to the three bureaus.

Whatever you decide, please accept my grateful appreciation for your consideration. I look forward to hearing from you soon.

Sincerely,

Sample FCBA Evidence Request

Date: _____

Creditor Name
Creditor Address

Re: Acc. # _____

CERTIFIED MAIL; RETURN RECEIPT REQUESTED

Dear Sir or Madam,

I have obtained a copy of my credit report, and it shows late payments on the above account. Specifically, it states that I was (here describe what the credit report shows, for example, that you were XX days late on a payment). This is very disturbing, and it is doing serious damage to my credit rating.

As you know, you are required by law to make sure that my bills are accurate. You must send my bills to my correct address, change my address when I request it, promptly and accurately record any payments I make, and apply late fees and charges only when payments are, in fact, late.

I hereby request that you take the following steps to remedy the situation:

- Send me a notarized statement attesting to your compliance with all provisions of the Fair Credit Billing Act with respect to my account.

- Provide documentary evidence of my indebtedness for all charges for which you claim I made late payment.

- Provide documentary evidence of timely billing and timely posting of all payments made on this account, whether or not you claim they were late, from the date the account was opened through the present.

If you cannot provide the statements and documentary evidence required, then I insist that you delete all negative references from your reports to Experian, Equifax and TransUnion. **If I do not receive all three items itemized above within the period prescribed by law, I will expect to receive written notification that you have, in fact, made the required deletions from your reports and that you have removed from my file any reference to the disputed late payments.**

Please attend to my requests promptly. Time is of the essence.

To verify my ID and my address, I am enclosing copies of (here describe a government-issued identification, such as a state drivers' license or a passport) and a recent (here describe a utility bill, such as a phone bill or an electric bill, that shows your current mailing address).

Sincerely yours,

_____

Sample Validation Request 1

Date: _____

Debt Collector Name: _____
Debt Collector Address: _____

Re: Creditor Name: _____
      Acc. # _____

CERTIFIED MAIL; RETURN RECEIPT REQUESTED

Dear Sir or Madam,

I recently learned that my credit report reflects a negative entry concerning the above creditor and account.

I hereby request that you provide me with written validation of this debt in accordance with the provisions of The Fair Debt Collection Practices Act. This validation must include the name and address of the original creditor, documentation obtained from the creditor proving that I have a legal obligation to pay, documentation proving that you have the legal authority to collect, and all other notices required by law. If you cannot provide the validation required, then you must

1. Remove from your files any negative reference concerning this account,

2. Immediately notify Experian, Equifax and TransUnion that your previous communications regarding this account were incorrect and ask them to remove any negative reference from my credit report.

I also require that you communicate with me only in writing, and only at the address provided above. You may not contact me by phone at any time, for any reason.

To verify my ID and my address, I am enclosing copies of (here describe a government-issued identification, such as a state drivers' license or a passport) and a recent (here describe a utility bill, such as a phone bill or an electric bill, that shows your current mailing address).

Sincerely yours,

Wollman FTC Opinion Letter

UNITED STATES OF AMERICA
FEDERAL TRADE COMMISSION
WASHINGTON, D.C. 20580

Division of Credit Practices
Bureau of Consumer Protection

March 10, 1993

Jeffrey S. Wollman
Vice President and Controller
Retrieval Masters Creditors Bureau, Inc.
1261 Broadway
New York, New York 10001

Dear Mr. Wollman:

This is in response to your letter of February 9, 1993 to David Medine regarding the type of verification required by Section 809(b) of the Fair Debt Collection Practices Act. You ask whether a collection agency for a medical provider will fulfill the requirements of that Section if it produces "an itemized statement of services rendered to a patient on its own computer from information provided by the medical institution. . ." in response to a request for verification of the debt. You also ask who is responsible for mailing the verification to the consumer.

The statute requires that the debt collector obtain verification of the debt and mail it to the consumer (emphasis mine). Because one of the principal purposes of this Section is to help consumers who have been misidentified by the debt collector or who dispute the amount of the debt, it is important that the verification of the identity of the consumer and the amount of the debt be obtained directly from the creditor. Mere itemization of what the debt collector already has does not accomplish this purpose. As stated above, the statute requires the debt collector, not the creditor, to mail the verification to the consumer.

Your interest in writing is appreciated. Please be aware that since this is only the opinion of Commission staff, the Commission itself is not bound by it.

Sincerely,

John F. LeFevre
Attorney
Division of Credit Practices

Cass FTC Opinion Letter

UNITED STATES OF AMERICA
FEDERAL TRADE COMMISSION
WASHINGTON, D.C. 20580

Federal Trade Commission

December 23, 1997

Robert G. Cass
Compliance Counsel
Commercial Financial Services, Inc.
2448 E. 81st Street, Suite 5500
Tulsa, OK 74137-4248

Dear Mr. Cass:

Mr. Medine has asked me to reply to your letter of October 28, 1997, concerning the circumstances under which a debt collector may report a "charged-off debt" to a consumer reporting agency under the enclosed Fair Debt Collection Practices Act. In that letter, you pose four questions, which I set out below with our answers.

I. "Is it permissible under the FDCPA for a debt collector to report charged-off debts to a consumer reporting agency during the term of the 30-day validation period detailed in Section 1692g?" Yes. As stated in the Commission's Staff Commentary on the FDCPA (copy enclosed), a debt collector may accurately report a debt to a consumer reporting agency within the thirty day validation period (p. 50103). We do not regard the action of reporting a debt to a consumer reporting agency as inconsistent with the consumer's dispute or verification rights under § 1692g.

II. "Is it permissible under the FDCPA for a debt collector to report, or continue to report, a consumer's charged-off debt to a consumer reporting agency after the debt collector has received, but not responded to, a consumer's written dispute during the 30-day validation period detailed in § 1692g?" As you know, Section 1692g(b) requires the debt collector to cease collection of the debt at issue if a written dispute is received within the 30-day validation period until verification is obtained. Because we believe that reporting a charged-off debt to a consumer reporting agency, particularly at this stage of the collection process, constitutes "collection activity" on the part of the collector, our answer to your question is No. Although the FDCPA is unclear on this point, we believe the reality is that debt collectors use the reporting mechanism as a tool to persuade consumers to pay, just like dunning letters and telephone calls. Of course, if a dispute is received after a debt has been reported to a consumer reporting agency, the debt collector is obligated by Section 1692e(8) to inform the consumer reporting agency of the dispute.

III. "Is it permissible under the FDCPA to cease collection of a debt rather than respond to a written dispute from a consumer received during the 30-day validation period?" Yes. There is nothing in the FDCPA that requires a debt collector to continue collecting a debt after a written dispute is received. Further, there is nothing in the FDCPA that requires a response to a written dispute if the debt collector chooses to abandon its collection effort with respect to the debt at issue. See Smith v. Transworld Systems, Inc., 953 F.2d 1025, 1032 (6th Cir. 1992).

IV. "Would the following action by a debt collector constitute continued collection activity under §1692g(b): reporting a charged-off consumer debt to a consumer reporting agency as disputed in accordance with § 1692e(8), when the debt collector became aware of the dispute when the consumer sent a written dispute to the debt collector during the 30-day validation period, and no verification of the debt has been provided by the debt collector?" Yes. As stated in our answer to Question II, we view reporting to a consumer reporting agency as a collection activity prohibited by § 1692g(b) after a written dispute is received and no verification has been provided. Again, however, a debt collector must report a dispute received after a debt has been reported under §1692e(8).

I hope this is responsive to your request.

Sincerely,

John F. LeFevre
Attorney

Sample Investigation Request

Date: _____

Credit Reporting Agency:_____
Credit Reporting Agency Address: _____

Re: Notice of Dispute of Negative References

CERTIFIED MAIL; RETURN RECEIPT REQUESTED

Dear Sir or Madam,

I recently received from you a copy of my credit report. Enclosed is a copy of that report, with certain negative references circled. I am writing to dispute each of these circled items:

1. (here describe the first circled reference exactly as it appears on the credit report)

2. (here describe the second circled reference exactly as it appears on the credit report)

Item 1 above is inaccurate (or incomplete) because (here describe why the reference is either not accurate or is not complete).

Item 2 above is inaccurate (or incomplete) because (here describe why the reference is either not accurate or is not complete).

I ask that you investigate these disputed negative references. If your investigation discloses that the references are inaccurate or incomplete, or that they cannot be verified, then please delete these items from my report as required by The Fair Credit Reporting Act.

To assist you in your investigation, I am enclosing copies of the following documents (here describe any documents that support your position):

1. _____
2. _____
3. _____

To verify my ID and my address, I am also enclosing copies of (here describe a government-issued identification, such as a state drivers' license or a passport) and a recent (here describe a utility bill, such as a phone bill or an electric bill, that shows your current mailing address).

Sincerely yours,

_____

Sample Validation Request 2

Date: _____

Debt Collector Name: _____
Debt Collector Address: _____

Re: Creditor Name: _____
     Acc. # _____

CERTIFIED MAIL; RETURN RECEIPT REQUESTED

Dear Sir or Madam,

I recently received a letter from you in which you claim that I owe money on the account referenced above. A copy of that letter is enclosed for your reference.

I hereby request that you provide me with written validation of this debt in accordance with the provisions of The Fair Debt Collection Practices Act. This validation must include the name and address of the original creditor, documentation proving that I have a legal obligation to pay, documentation proving that you have the right to collect it, and all other notices required by law.

I also require that you communicate with me only in writing, and only at the address provided above. You may not contact me by phone at any time, for any reason.

To verify my ID and my address, I am enclosing copies of (here describe a government-issued identification, such as a state drivers' license or a passport) and a recent (here describe a utility bill, such as a phone bill or an electric bill, that shows your current mailing address).

Sincerely yours,

_____